MW00989202

THE LAST DECADENT

A Study Of Brian Jones

◆

Jeremy Reed

credits

the last decadent
a study of brian jones
by:
jeremy reed
ISBN 1 871592 71 2
© jeremy reed 1999
first published July 2nd 1999 by:
creation books
london • san francisco
this edition © creation books 1999
design/layout/typesetting:
pcp international, bradley davis
photo credits:
all photos of brian jones by courtesy of rex features

author's acknowledgements

the author would like to express huge gratitude to kate o'leary for typing the text; richard lovett and the spirit for making information available to me; nicholas fitzgerald for his sensitive portrait of brian; john robinson for being integral to all my work; and my publisher, james williamson, for unfailing encouragement and support.

written at the hampstead tea rooms, london, november 1998 — february 1999.

This book is for
My mother for encouraging me in this work
Holly Elsdon for her love of Brian's shirts
Richard Lovett for his devotion to Brian
Pat Andrews for speaking of Brian with such love

CONTENTS

THE LAST DECADENT

"The road of excess leads to the palace of wisdom"
—William Blake

FOREWORD

Let's not talk of the millennium, although doom and decay, and deliriously frightening good times figure in this story. United here are two fleeting wraiths from the past and the present, their link to me, perhaps, only pretty shirts, velvet and a love of chaos. Jeremy Reed, I talk to on the phone; Brian Jones, I listen to from a greater distance. Apparently, he was a difficult chap: I never saw that side.

The first time I met him, I was in John Lee Hooker's back-up band, a privilege. It was the winter of 1966, and we were doing a gig at The Bag O' Nails, a second-rung of cool, late-night, West-end dive. A few minutes into the set, Mr Jones walked in, not a difficult man to spot in a crowd. Suddenly, I was nervous; I tried to forget he was there. At one point, I put on my bottleneck and looked out into the darkness; he flashed me a wink. "Oh, dear," I thought.

He was there backstage, of course, talking to John Lee. Gone was the "we-can-piss-anywhere" attitude, gone the beautiful and arrogant dandy: he was a blues-fan, just like me, almost a nerd. Later we went to the bar, waffled on about guitars and girls, deep into the night, the usual muso stuff. I never thought I'd see him again.

A while later, I'm shopping for clothes in the King's Road – Dandy Fashions. I take the world's most wonderful psychedelic shirt to the desk, asking for a smaller size. Brian holds up the same shirt: "This what you want?" My size. He passes it over. "It's paid for," he says, and walks out.

Overwhelmingly, it is his look and presence for which Brian Jones is remembered. But, "Paint It Black" remains, perhaps, the only successful use of sitar in Western pop music, avoiding with elegance the ghastly trap of travel-agent orientalisms. His slide-guitar on "Little

Red Rooster" unveils a melodic subtlety and sweetness of tone that puts him up there with Earl Hooker and Tampa Red, this at a time when us Anglo whiteboys were only just discovering the blues, and mostly playing it in an embarrassingly ham-fisted way. One might think it a happy accident in the studio, but I don't believe in accidents.

This was borne out in the sessions at Cotchford, when I rehearsed with Brian and his new band, working in the living room he had converted into a studio. I remember both our joint love of playing blues riffs, and the exploitation he suffered from the less salubrious people on his property.

The drooling moron that pushed Brian Jones under has gone to where he belongs. Do demons molest him with red-hot pokers while Brian laughs? I rather hope so, and hope, also, that we all find our peace after the burning flames.

—Martin Stone

INTRODUCTION: **LADY JANE**

"Brian was the only woman he ever really loved."

—Suki Potier

Brian Jones knew how to sit like a lady. Dressed in a dark blue shirt snowed with white polka dots, and with his blond fringe effeminately cut to the eyebrows, his live footage appearance on *Top Of The Pops* in 1966 was the classic image of sixties androgyny. In fact it's almost possible to forget the four remaining members of the Rolling Stones and their individual contributions to "Lady Jane", so powerful is the auric magnitude that Jones commands as he sits cross-legged with his dulcimer, and totally concentrated on his instrument. And even if the audience were unaware of the dichotomised politics at play within the band, the songwriting team of Jagger and Richards having succeeded in usurping Jones's seminal musical influences, then Brian already looked like a man set apart from his colleagues.

Jones's appearance, even in the fashion-obsessed extravaganza that characterised sixties culture, was marked by an inherently realised sexual ambidexterity that placed him at the forefront of gender-deconstruction. It was not for nothing that his chosen sobriquet was Mr. Shampoo, and Brian, who forbade anybody including lovers to touch his highlighted hair, guarded the latter as a sacred fetish. Jones's live-in lover at the time, Anita Pallenberg, with whom he shared an opulent apartment at 1 Courtfield Road, South Kensington, has told of how she was only permitted to trim Brian's hair using three mirrors, and by a slow-motion effect that allowed him to constantly review her progress.

Brian it seems was an aesthete, an asthmatic, a schizoid-paranoid individual deeply wounded by his upbringing, and by sensibility a decadent. Decadence as a cultural phenomenon has a long and perverse history, and the individuals who subscribe to its unnatural dictates are invariably those who feel uncomfortable with reality. According to Marianne Faithfull in her autobiography *Year One*: "Today you would put anybody in Brian's shaky condition straight into hospital. But we never even considered it. I don't honestly think it crossed anybody's mind to 'seek professional help'. And he, of course, would never have accepted it."

Decadence is an irrepressible gene. It was present in the sassy genome shared by the late Roman Emperors, and manifested itself in the perversely deviant lives of Caligula, Commodus, Nero and Heliogabalus. Heliogabalus, who decorated his blond hair with pearls, cross-dressed and wore heavy make-up, was legendary for his spectacular sodomitical orgies. Wearing a solar tiara he would preside over rites involving bacchic music, and the instruments used were a diverse mix of cymbals, lyres, tambours, flutes, harps and sistrums. Heliogabalus's concerts may be seen as the template for the pop festivals which begun in the sixties, and have continued down the decades to represent a subversion of order. A festival permits the collective to liberate their psychosexual energies within a sympathetic precinct. There's a case for arguing that Heliogabalus was the prototypical pop star. As an Emperor he was adverse to war, had women replace men in the Senate, advocated theatre and music, and turned his attention to the arts. He was in many ways looking across the centuries towards a pacifist, sex-liberated 1960s pop culture.

Heliogabalus and Brian Jones share a decadent interface. I suspect they would have liked each other, and Brian, dressed in a purple silk gown, would have played flute or harp at the foot of the Emperor's couch. Heliogabalus too met an early death, murdered in the palace latrines by soldiers outraged at the youth's flaunting of gay sex.

Brian Jones's numerous biographers have all failed to point up a case for the musician's inheritance of a decadent genealogy. Brian with his sophisticated voice and refined manners appeared to his lippy streetwise colleagues as a dysfunctional poseur who had little grasp on practical reality. It has been suggested, although never fully authenticated that Brian was an epileptic, and there seems little doubt from his medical history that much of his life was spent attempting to hide the symptoms of chronic anxiety from his public. He was fragile and hypersensitive and ill-suited to the demands of fame. Whatever his formative conception of a possible future for the Rolling Stones, he could never have counted on the band's escalating rise to megastardom. Brian may have fantasised about being dramatically haloed for his skills as a bluesman, but when the dream was transformed to a reality in the early part of the sixties he grew terrified of the consequences of over-exposure to the public. His paranoia had him feel like an angel-fish spotlit in an aquarium. He took refuge in drugs and alcohol to chemically screen himself from media intrusion, and from the almost vampirical invasion of his private life by fans. According to Marianne Faithfull and to all of those who were close to Brian at the time, his mental state deteriorated after he had begun to experiment with drugs. Faithfull writes: "Brian was a mess – a neurasthenic and hypersensitive. Twitchy. The slightest thing would set him off. He would let things gnaw at him and he would brood. This paranoiac condition worsened, naturally, on acid."

Brian's pathology, with or without him realising it, extended to the decadent pantheon of ruined sensibilities. By the eighteenth century decadence could boast amongst its famous devotees the Marquis de Sade, and the English eccentric William Beckford, author of *Vathek*, who after being ostracised for homosexual offences built himself the fantastic Fonthill Abbey, and retired there to engage in a private world not so dissimilar in its preoccupations to those pursued by Michael Jackson at Neverland.

But it was in France that decadence first became a psychological issue, and in 1770 we find Voltaire writing to his friend La Harpe with the pronouncement: "Don't hope to re-establish good taste, we are in a time of the most horrible decadence." It was a theme to be taken up by the Marquis de Sade who perversely affirmed: "The happiest state will always be that in which depravity of manners and morals is most universal." Sixty years later we are to find Flaubert writing: "I love above all the display of vegetation growing upon old ruins; this embrace of nature coming rapidly to bury the work of man the moment his hand is no longer there to defend it, fills me with deep joy."

And there were other advocates of moral ruins. The poems and short stories of Edgar Allan Poe with their emphasis on a necrophilic subtext in which death is seen as preferable to life, were written by an opium and alcohol addicted author. Poe married his cousin Virginia Clemm when she was thirteen, the secret marriage in Baltimore being legitimised the following year in Virginia. With his nerves stripped to bare wiring as a consequence of attempting to support himself by writing, Poe's life devolved into a dipsomaniacal series of catastrophes. Contracted to do a series of lectures and poetry readings, Poe's black-suited stage presence attracted audiences, no matter the likelihood of his either being too out of it to appear, or fortified with the excuse that he had lost his lecture notes. Although the link is a tenuous one, we can find in Poe's paranoid stage image the beginnings of an audience being attracted to a substances-damaged performer. A century later Brian Jones was to assert a similar attraction to audiences instinctually aware of his vulnerability. The idea of the artist living on the edge of breakdown had reached the pop ethos via the blues and jazz world in which artists like Bessie Smith and Billie Holiday had visibly manifested serious drug habits. It should be remembered that Brian's early musical polarisation was to the sound of the Chicago Blues, and as a teenager living in Cheltenham he collected records by Sonny Boy Williamson, a friend of Elmore James, T Bone Walker and Jimmy Reed. That the blues, or more specifically rhythm & blues was a music expressive of cultural protest correspondingly implied that the musicians drawn to it were invariably associated with substance abuse. The proponents of rhythm & blues nurtured a grievance in psyche against a conventionally structured capitalist ethos. They were, like Brian, non-conformists, and used their music to express a statement of individual freedom. In this respect they were proponents of decadence who highlighted their social difference by adopting lifestyles considered angular to the status quo. Other artists who featured prominently in Brian's pantheon of blues heroes were Elmore James, Bo Diddley, John Lee Hooker, Muddy Waters, Howlin' Wolf, Alexis Korner, Blind Boy Fuller and Humphrey Lyttleton.

As an aesthetic genre decadence is largely associated with the literature and art of mid-nineteenth-century France. It was Gautier who first used the epithet "decadent" to describe Charles Baudelaire. Baudelaire, the author of *Les Fleurs Du Mal* (1850), would after the prosecution for obscenity of his seminally infamous book of poems come to be considered as the prototypically aesthetic decadent. With the intention of shocking the bourgeois out of what he considered to be an inveterately commonplace sensibility he took to dyeing his hair green, or to shaving his head like a criminal. Baudelaire declared war on utilitarianism, and cultivated a code of dandifying the artist at the expense of the public. An impoverished aristocrat attempting to live off a frozen trust-fund, and a man who considered work to be a vilification of spirit, Baudelaire developed an incurable opium habit, and used his addiction to further separate himself from the reality he so despised.

Brian Jones was a child of Baudelairean sympathies. He inherited via the decadent tradition an attraction to the occult powers of satanism, a love of hashish and a variety of mind-altering substances, an interest in Eastern music, and a propensity for the sybaritic luxury advocated by Baudelaire and his successors like J.K. Huysmans and Oscar Wilde. Baudelaire's dynamic was the imagination as it transforms morbid psychology. His life and art were devoted to excavating psychic ruins. "Usefulness to the community has always seemed to me a most hideous thing in a man," he was to write in his *Intimate Journals*. Baudelaire defended the individual against the collective, and his disgust for mindless totalitarianism had him take refuges in an increasing solitude. "There are people who can entertain themselves only in a herd," he was to write in his *Journals*. "The true hero finds his entertainment in solitude."

Baudelaire, who comprised the beginnings of the modern sensibility, was also known as the Paris Prowler. He would stalk prostitutes on his nocturnal peregrinations of the city, but never enter into relations with them. The disappointment generated by his turbulent relationship with the mulatto Jeanne Duval, in itself a social scandal at the time, seems to have hardened his character into that of an asexual misogynist. "The boring thing about love-making," he was to write, "is that it's a crime for which one cannot dispense with an accomplice."

The more aesthetic the sensibility the greater the tendency towards bisexual orientation. Baudelaire's pronounced anima and his distinctly feminine traits would have encouraged him in more sympathetic times to same-sex relations. The same could be said of Brian Jones. Brian, who openly wore costume jewellery picked up from Saks Fifth Avenue in New York, and who was the advocate of white shoes and lace blouses for men, was of his own admission bisexual. Jones told his friend Nicholas Fitzgerald, a Guinness Brewery heir that, "A lot of people in rock are ambidextrous as far as sex is concerned. They're just too uptight to admit it or practise it."

Anita Pallenberg was to enforce Brian's ambiguous statement by claiming that he had gone to bed with Mick Jagger. In Geoffrey Giuliano's *Paint It Black*, the author quotes Pallenberg as saying: "I only know that Brian did break up a lot of things by actually going to bed with Mick. And I think Mick always resented him for having fallen for it. In later years there have been rumours about Mick being gay, but then it was as if Brian violated Mick's privacy by revealing his weak side."

The successor to Baudelaire's role as premier decadent was the novelist Joris-Karl Huysmans, whose novel *A Rebours* ("Against Nature"), proved to be the quintessential synthesis of morbid pathologies. Des Esseintes, the protagonist of Huysmans' novel, embodies a compendium of synaesthetic neuroses. His systematic experimentation with all sensory stimuli extends to a love of art, perfumes, exotic flowers, jewels, food and wines, books and unnatural sex, and incorporates a program of postulating beauty, no matter how debased, as an absolute.

Des Esseintes has sufficient means to withdraw from the world and luxuriate in his chosen life of epicurean sensation. His gravitation towards everything corrupt, and his pursuit of self-indulgent hedonism make him the blueprint of the decadent traits of sixties rock musicians like Brian Jones. And if Des Esseintes was able by virtue of his privileges to exclude reality from his life, then so too was Brian by way of the wealth he accumulated as a member of the Rolling Stones.

Decadence, as I have stated, is a gene. Brian may not have read *Against Nature*, but the sensibility designed by the book is one that he unconsciously inherited. There's a Des Esseintes in every generation, and Brian Jones embodied the decadent hero's characteristics for the youth who comprised a gender-subversive sixties. He was somehow the personification of that ideal at a particular moment in history. And like Des Esseintes, Brian's inner world was the metaphor for his external presence. Brian's clothes mirrored the predominantly feminine image he had of himself. Des Esseintes in Huysmans' novel is portrayed as wearing a bunch of Parma violets at his throat instead of a cravat, and one could imagine Brian approving of this ostentatious gesture.

Des Esseintes is additionally portrayed as wasted from the cultivation of unnatural pleasures. Largely disinterested in the apparent banality of heterosexual encounters, he extends his sexual repertoire by opportunistically initiating a schoolboy into gay experience. Des Esseintes never questions his need of sensory kicks, or reflects on the outcome of what is described as an aberrant relationship. The youth in question is possessed of long black hair, a small mouth like a cherry, and is holding a school-book in his hand. This incident could equally have been a sixties scenario for someone like Brian. The essentially vitiated and amoral sensibility spotlit by Huysmans in *Against Nature*, was the one inherited by the twentieth-century, and its manifestations have informed on various levels such disparate phenomena as the Weimar Republic and Nazism, aspects of music and drug culture in the sixties, and punk rock.

If you look at the photograph of the Rolling Stones originally intended as the album cover for *Beggar's Banquet*, from a theatrical shoot taken at Sarum Chase stately home, then Brian is the one whose decadence appears less affected. Sitting to the right of a table on which a banquet has been spread, Brian is framed holding a wine goblet with feminine delicacy, his blond hair setting him apart from the group poseurs who would otherwise be out of place in such decadent surroundings. He looks a natural amongst the stuffed animals arranged as props, the candlesticks, the dishes loaded with black grapes, the broodingly oppressive atmospherics generated by the room, and the striking occult head and shoulders placed as a prop on the loaded table.

Decadence as a posture reached England via the Romantic legacy of the flagrantly perverse and uncompromising Lord Byron. Byron boasted openly of having conducted an incestuous relationship with his half-sister, and something of his legendary sadism may have owed its origins to his physical deformity. Living on credit to allow for his aristocratic tastes, Byron pursued a life of sexual profligacy, much of his libidinal energies being channelled into casual sex with men. Mario Praz has put it succinctly by writing: "It was in transgression that Byron found his own life-rhythm." Byron delighted in destroying others, and the intensity of his misogynist dynamic was fed by an equally vicious alcoholism. Byron would have delighted in the moral subversion associated with the Rolling Stones, and given a century might well have found himself as the band's sixth member. Byron lived without restraint and capitalised on the privilege of a title in order to secure credit. In his life as a member of the Rolling Stones, Brian Jones was regularly to find himself overdrawn, or in lieu of unpaid salary, and like Byron he was able to use his name as a means to maintaining a steady cash flow.

Any account of decadence in relation to Brian Jones would be incomplete without bringing into the arena the names of Count Eric Stenbock and Oscar Wilde. Eric Stenbock, who is best remembered for his vampire stories collected in *Studies Of Death* (1894), was born in Kolk in Estonia, before the family moved to Withdeane Hall, near Brighton. Stenbock, who left Oxford without a degree, became exceedingly wealthy after his inheritance in 1885. Occupying a London house in Sloane Terrace, the Count devoted himself to creating the sort of artificial microcosm inhabited by Des Esseintes in Huysmans' *Against Nature*. Stenbock housed a menagerie, and visitors to the house remembered a pet monkey, a toad called Fatima, pythons, and a variety of parakeets and tropical birds. The Count, who regularly smoked opium, and who was a self-destructive alcoholic would dine off roast peacock served on a coffin acting as a table. A notorious homosexual, he would appear in public with a life-size male doll on his arm. A contemporary vignette of Stenbock, tells of how before entering a room, "he paused, drew out a little gold vial of scent from his pocket, scented his finger-tips and passed them through his hair before greeting his hostess."

Like Brian Jones, Stenbock was known for his long blond hair. It was a feature which enhanced his femininity. He is described as small, with blue doll-like eyes. Stenbock, although he achieved little of literary merit, has left an indelible fingerprint on the androgynous psyche.

No account of the formative influences of decadence on sixties musicians like Brian Jones could dispense with the figure of Oscar Wilde as prototypical underworld rebel. For all of Wilde's erudition as a classicist and his lacerating satirical wit as a playwright, it is as the underground novelist who wrote *The Picture Of Dorian Gray* that he is most remembered. Wilde, the aesthetic sophisticate and sexual outlaw, despised the middle classes for their social convention. Courting defiance through his openly gay friendship with Lord Alfred Douglas, and subverting standards by dining with rent boys at Kettners in Soho, Wilde delighted in living on the cutting edge. He described his nocturnal entertainment as "feasting with panthers". Wilde, as much as Brian Jones was to do later, found in decadence a mode of protest against a middle-class upbringing. Both men affected camp dress as a defensive screen between themselves and reality.

"I consider," wrote Wilde, "that for any man of culture to accept the standard of his age is a form of the grossest immorality." Much has been made of Wilde's aesthetic decadence, within a particular period, the *fin de siècle*, but little has been made of his subversive over-reach which has travelled down the century, via the underground, to influence minority culture. *Dorian Gray* was the first openly gay British novel, and as such the book created a scandal. So profound were the social repercussions established by the novel, that pages of it were used as evidence against Wilde in his trial. Wilde reacted against the moral straitjacketing of a Victorian ethos, in the way that Brian Jones and his musical compatriots incepted sexual freedom in the sixties.

Wilde, with his Byronic costume, his astrakhan coats, green carnations worn as buttonholes, his Neronian hairstyle done for him by Pascal under the Grand Hotel in Paris, his love of a perfume called *lilas blanc*, his sweeping Ascot hats and pink shirts, shocked society by his presentation of the artist as decadent.

In the 1960s Brian Jones was to delight in a passion for hats and fur coats, not so dissimilar to those worn by Oscar. In a memorable shot of the Rolling Stones taken in Green Park, London, in 1967, Brian appears unforgettably in a Wildean costume of red and black striped trousers, a black velvet Regency jacket, a loud silk tie and a white hat. It's typically Novemberish, the leaves are almost down, and the slightly frozen stance of the group suggests figures slightly dampened by the rainy chill. Jagger has his collar turned up, and all five members of the Rolling Stones seem conscious that they are being arrested at a particular moment in time. For all of his inimitably radiant charisma as a performer, Mick Jagger is glaringly overshadowed by Brian's presence and sartorial elegance. It was Brian who attracted the Stones's girl fanbase, and it was his early feminine posturing on stage that Jagger was later to vampirise in the evolution of his androgynous stage act.

Oscar Wilde was by his disregard for social and sexual conventions, and by his artistic appearance aimed at distinguishing himself from the masses, the originator of the pop ethos. Oscar would have delighted in being called a pop star, and his blend of sassy camp would have been readily sanctioned by the rock milieu. As it was, he found himself imprisoned and later ostracised for being the *zeitgeist* informing gay liberation. No other nineteenth century writer would have dared proclaim with such unequivocal temerity that: "Sin is the only real colour-element left in modern life." And that, "I represent to you all the sins you have never had the courage to commit." Wilde's notions were considered scandalous then, and are no better received by the establishment today.

There's the memorable incident in *The Picture Of Dorian Gray*, when Dorian goes to a ball in a dress "covered with five hundred and sixty pearls". Prosecution at Wilde's trial revealed that he consorted with transvestites, and amongst them Alfred Taylor, who like Wilde was sent down. Cross-dressing as a gender statement appealed to the Rolling Stones. It was Jagger who in the early sixties would camp it up indoors at Edith Grove in a shocking-blue linen housecoat, waving his hands in the air like a queenish diva. Apart from the blues foundation to their raw early sound, much of the initial fascination asserted by the Rolling Stones lay in the androgynous image projected by Jones and Jagger. Both wore their hair long at a time when it was considered outrageous for men to adopt women's hairdos. The two also developed a love of soft angora and lambswool crew-neck and polo-neck sweaters when such garments were almost exclusive to female fashion.

In 1966, when the Rolling Stones shocked the media by appearing in drag on the colour sleeve of their single, "Have You Seen Your Mother Baby, Standing In The Shadows?" Brian was presented as a blonde WAAF officer pouting smoke-rings at the camera, while prominently pointing up his falsies. The photo session was filmed by Peter Whitehead in a New York backstreet off Third Avenue. Two decades later Mick Jagger was to say of the event: "Well, it's just a thing about English men. We don't need much encouragement to dress up. I mean, if you've got friends over for the weekend and you get bored and want to dress up as women and go down to the pub, that's all right. You don't need more than that one time asking." For the poses of the Whitehead photo session, Jagger adopted the name Sarah for the day, while Brian became Flossie.

There's a disputed picture of Oscar Wilde dragging it up as Salome, and men in frocks would certainly have been an issue at hand colouring Wilde's visits to Alfred Taylor's rooms in Little College Street, London. Wilde understood both the necessity to shock bourgeois complacency, as well as the insignificance of the gesture, when he wrote: "It's not difficult to walk down Piccadilly carrying a lily; what is difficult is to make people think I did." Much of the paradoxical dilemma associated with the glamour of being a pop star, and yet being denied artistic credibility as a consequence of that role, is encapsulated by Wilde's witticism. The shock-waves injected into a gender-frozen post-fifties British culture by the Rolling Stones had an older generation attempt to discredit their artistic relevance. The Stones were seen as an infectious threat to male identity. Brian's effeminacy, despite his documented relationships with women, was viewed by the homophobic as a statement advocating gay rights.

Clothes are confrontational, particularly if they are worn to externalise the wearer's identification with anima or animus. Wilde's dress had the authorities identify him as homosexual, in the way that the police harassed Brian Jones because his appearance was thought to be synonymous with doing drugs. Both men were marked because they dared to differ. In the attempt to apply a rationale to every form of deviance, society gives labels to the unconventional. Oscar Wilde was branded a pederast and Brian Jones a druggie degenerate. Both individuals were targeted by the London police and brought to trial by popular climate. No allowance in either case was given to their respective artistic sensibilities. Brian was twice set up and brought to court on account of minor drug charges, in the way that an authoritarian society tried Wilde three times before being successful in bringing a conviction.

Because the law refused to proscribe lesbianism, women in suits have been left alone over the years. Marlene Dietrich wore a black tuxedo in her first American film, *Morocco* (1930), repeated the act by wearing a white one in *Blond Venus* (1932), and boasted a naval uniform for her part in *Seven Sinners* (1940). Garbo who wore male attire in the title role in *Queen Christina* (1933), was instrumental to popularising women's wearing of trousers. The pantheon of women dressed as men is an inexhaustible one, and twentieth-century archetypes of the genre include Gertrude Stein, Radclyffe Hall, Romaine Brooks, Vita Sackville-West, Violet Trefusis, the eccentric Joe Carstairs, and the impeccably suited singer kd lang.

Drag has always been part of the British theatrical tradition, and in Wilde's *fin de siècle* London drag was vulgarised for populist forms of music hall and pantomime. The role created for the Pantomime Dame was that of a burlesque man in drag. Waspish humour, crackling repartee, the persona of an essentially frilly female, and an ability to convince in that role were some of the aspects needed to enhance the repertory of a Dame. For Wilde's generation, it was Dan Leno who provided drag entertainment, and so convincing was he as a female artiste, that the audience forgot he was a man imitating a woman.

Drag acts have always been an entertainment feature at gay clubs, but as such were confined to a sympathetic milieu. The cross over in London came in the 1950s when drag began to prove a popular attraction in some straight pubs such as Stockwell's Vauxhall Tavern and Camden's Black Cap. These pubs were quickly taken over by a gay clientele, but the idea of men in frocks outside a theatrical precinct would have entertained the violation of social taboo. Men would not in the 1950s have dared appear in the costumes that Brian was to wear with impunity a decade later in the adventurously flamboyant 1960s. What the sixties provided by way of a fashion statement was the notion that predominantly straight men could explore aspects of their femininity without implying that they were homosexual. As the decade advanced, so a male generation realised that looking feminine increased their attraction to women. By the end of the decade, and ironically at the Hyde Park memorial concert for Brian Jones, Mick Jagger was to appear wearing a white smock designed by Mr. Fish. Queenishly mincing on to the stage, Jagger was to use the allure of camp accoutrements to convince an audience that he was sexually dangerous in an ambivalent way. The songs may have been aggressively heterosexual in their raunchy bar-room polarisation, but Jagger's demeanour on stage was decadently effeminate.

Brian Jones's psychology was involutedly complex, and so too undoubtedly were his psychic components of gender. His friend, Alexis Korner, has spoken of the knotty, introverted layers that existed in Brian's psyche. "Brian was always trying to figure things out," Korner tells us. "I presume he got to the point where he asked himself questions and couldn't understand his answers. He tied himself in a knot, a very brittle knot. I think if you would have untied the knot, the rope would have fallen to pieces, in millions of little fragments."

Korner's metaphor for Brian's increasingly contracted introversion, is a good one. We should remember that Brian was asthmatic, and as asthma is characterised by the inability to let go and exhale, so the illness perfectly suited the subject. Brian had quickly discovered that he could trust no one in the music industry, and so his directional impulse as a sensitive person was to turn inward and find preoccupation with a world of self-generated fantasies. Brian's relation to the feminine clothes he wore was dictated far more by inner compulsions than it was fashion awareness. For Brian, the need to emphasise his process of individuation was founded on deep feelings of separation from the collective. Brian would doubtless have gravitated to wearing feminine clothes even if the sixties had not occurred. As it was, the escalating galaxy of unisex boutiques that constellated London's Carnaby Street and the King's Road, provided Brian with a dazzling emporia from which he could dress to nurture his fantasies. As a fashion shopaholic he was also to draw on the Chelsea Antique Market as a source of additional inspiration to his multi-period tastes in costume. Jones's extremism in dressing up even led to him being photographed in a Nazi SS uniform, stamping on a doll, for the cover of a German periodical.

Still on the subject of decadence, Brian had other forebears like the English symbolist novelist Ronald Firbank, who painted his nails red in the 1920s, and was known to feed his goldfish pearls. There was Stephen Tennant, the one time lover of the poet Siegfried Sassoon, who from his andropausal middle-years dyed his hair pink and took to bed, and there was of course Quentin Crisp, the much vilified effigy for homophobics who resented men wearing makeup in public. There was a history of British eccentrics who cross-dressed, and Brian Jones's peacock flamboyance as the most obviously risqué feminine-dressed member of the Rolling Stones represented the continuity of a tradition in which men dressed as women were confronted by male hostility. But for those who dress up, the excitement lies in the danger implied by the risk. Both Jones and Jagger were regularly shredded by hysterical girl fans – the girls in this case appearing to avenge themselves on impostors to their sex. Crowed hysteria arising from early performances by Elvis Presley, the Beatles and the Rolling Stones was largely female-directed by a love-hate sisterhood who in a maenadic frenzy set about literally tearing the hair out of their so-called heroes, and ripping the shirts off their backs. Such retributive actions implied a psychic revival of the Erinnyes or Furies, and the sado-sexual undertones of girl fans left the vulnerable Brian Jones petrified by the fear of crowd assault. Jagger and Richards, as harder sensibilities, were better equipped to deal with audience violence, as the band became increasingly reliant for security on nefarious gofers and heavies. As the Stones dipped into the ranks of the quasi-criminal underworld for protection, so Brian found himself caught in a vicious circle of fearing alike invasive fans and the suspect nature of his minders. In his innately paranoid existence, Brian found himself able to trust nobody. He was rich, successful, but in his own mind hunted out of his skin. From all accounts Brian's minders and chauffeurs played on his weaknesses, and in the employ of the Stones' management they were instrumental in assisting the band to depose its gifted founder member.

Brian was in some ways the archetypal clown. If he dressed in a harlequin's costume, then he also took the extremes of being a feted pop star to desperate measures. He was in his youthful life searching for a vision, and perhaps in his last months the psychic foundations were laid towards his achieving a degree of self-realisation in terms of spiritual and creative aspirations. But as I have said, he was marked, in the way of the pariah. He was too serious an embodiment of sixties ideals. Fashion, drugs, unisexuality, rock music, pop art were all vitally new phenomena informing a decade which lacked the reflective experience which allows us to evaluate its merits in retrospect. Living in London, Brian was at the heart of turbulent psychosexual innovations, and as a natural rebel he embraced whatever cultural changes would help differentiate his generation from the conservative ideals upheld by his parents.

It was the Marquess of Queensberry who, outraged by Wilde's relations with his son, Lord Alfred Douglas, instigated the proceedings which were to bring Wilde to the criminal courts. Particularly telling was how he wrote of his son's association with Oscar Wilde: "I do not say you are it, but you look it, which is just as bad." An older, authoritarian generation thought similarly of Brian Jones and the Rolling Stones. Despite their heterosexual protestations, and in Brian's case he had already fathered four illegitimate children, there was the distinct media suspicion that both men were faggots. In terms of appearance Brian was unreservedly camp, by which I mean that his unacceptable characteristics provoked resentment in the orthodox. That he did his best to hide his mortification at being found vulnerable only served to increase the impulse within him to spectacularly self-destruct. Brian lived fast and partied compulsively to try and shut out not only the imminent terror of being made redundant by Jagger and Richards, but also the premonition of psychic catastrophe which seems to have hung over his life. People remember Brian's stay at 1 Courtfield Road as representing a continuous party. This mode of existence for a man who was by nature introverted and shy suggested a desperate attempt on Brian's part to silence the deeper promptings of his inner world. If camp is by definition, "the lie that tells the truth", then Brian seems to qualify as a devotee to this highly coloured mode of addressing life. One flick of his orange-blonde hair on stage professed the impenetrable secret he concealed from the world. In early Stones' performances, it was he rather than Jagger who would menace the audience by coming right to the edge of the stage, and with a cutie's gesture shake a tambourine at the crowd, as though inciting it to riot. Brian regularly bleached his blond hair to peroxide white, as though claiming he really was a blonde in the tradition of Mae West, Jean Harlow and Marilyn Monroe.

For the ancient Greeks blonde was the hair colour associated with the eternally youthful gods, and with their terrestrial counterparts – the heroes. Using saffron and henna as lighteners, Greek youth imitated the sunlight by going blonde. In ancient Rome, women wore blonde wigs as a sign that they were available, and the accoutrement was made fashionable by prostitutes. Vegetable and herbal rinses were used to bring about the desired highlighting, and these were often rinsed out on contact with the rain.

Brian Jones forms part of the twentieth-century's blonde ambition, a glamour fashion that dates from Mae West to Madonna at the time of her linking bottle blondes to icon worship. Ask anyone about Brian Jones, and they'll immediately visualise his blond curtains. The latter served to heighten his feminine-aspected mystique, and to accentuate the ambiguity of his sexual orientation. Brian shocked his early audiences by appearing blonde rather than the masculinized blond.

Wilde never peroxided his Neronian hairstyle, but in his sexual appetites he was like Brian Jones a Dionysian. It may be remembered that Dionysus is a bisexual god, an impulse that governs androgynous consciousness, and Wilde, who was moving psychically towards the integration of male and female, was governed by Dionysian propensities. Wilde's nocturnal energies, like Brian Jones's, were directed at sensory pleasure, and like all decadents both men lived by night. We can only speculate as to whether Wilde tried on blonde wigs at Alfred Taylor's flat in Little College Street. What is certain is that the morally uncompromising Oscar in part prepared the way for the sexual licentiousness enjoyed by the liberated 1960s. Wilde consorted with the underworld in the same way as Brian Jones went underground to look for dealers. Of his willingness to entertain rough trade, Wilde wrote: "People thought it dreadful of me to have entertained at dinner the evil things of life, and to have found pleasure in their company... it was like feasting with panthers. The danger was half the excitement."

Brian Jones's tragically hedonistic life perfectly subscribes to Wilde's sentiment that his highs came from testing the cutting edge. Brian's popularity as a musician meant that he lived in the camera's eye, and his *faux pas* became public knowledge. Brian's apartment at 1 Courtfield Road, which he was to share with his blonde look-alike, Anita Pallenberg, was suitably furnished to accommodate his decadent leanings. Incorporating a Moroccan theme into the interior design, Brian had the walls hung with embroidered Arabic rugs, while the floors were splashy with bright cushions constellating a centre piece hookah. Brian's friendship with the antique dealer, Christopher Gibbs, triggered in the pop star an insatiable passion to buy expensive antiques. The thirty-foot high rooms at Courtfield Road blended the acrid residue of dope smoke with notes of fragrant incense. A minstrel's gallery ran round the top of the rooms, and was hung with an assemblage of exotic instruments. The gallery was only accessible by climbing a rope ladder to meet with the elevation. Dressed in velvet, satin and lace, Brian must have taken the part of a twentieth-century minstrel as he sat above his guests, dragging on a top heavy joint.

In *Year One*, Marianne Faithfull has left her vivid recollections of aspects of life at Courtfield Road. One of these concerns Brian's love of dressing up. Of the passion that Jones shared with Pallenberg, Faithfull writes: "One of the best things about visiting Anita and Brian was watching them get ready to go out... Hours and hours were spent putting on clothes and taking them off again. Heaps of scarves, hats, shirts and boots flew out of drawers and trunks. Unending trying on of outfits, primping and sashaying... I would sit mesmerised for hours, watching them preening in the mirror, trying on each other's clothes. All roles and gender would evaporate in the narcissistic performances, where Anita would turn Brian into the Sun King, Francoise Hardy or the mirror image of herself."

But Faithfull amongst others describes how it was at Courtfield Road that Brian first became damaged by acid. Brian's naturally paranoid condition was exacerbated by the admixture of LSD to his chemistry. He would hallucinate, and imagine that the water pipes and the heating system were speaking to him of the dead. He would dialogue with his hallucinations, and then crumple up in a corner, nursing his depression. Acid left Brian transparent with vulnerability. He developed a compulsion to search the flat in the belief that somebody had planted drugs in a drawer or makeup container. Taking drugs amplified Brian's deep sense of guilt. On acid Brian would start writing songs that he was unable to complete. He would scribble lyric entries into notebooks, and begin recording and erasing, before finally wiping what he had committed to tape. His inferiority complex was the obstacle in terms of composition, and he seems to have dreaded the possibility of having his material rejected by the songwriting team of Jagger and Richards. By 1965 it had become *de rigueur* that the Stones recorded the infectiously catchy pop hits written by Jagger and Richards as the self-styled Glimmer Twins, and Brian was effectively reduced to being salaried as an instrumentalist to the band. The sense of rejection he felt at being relegated to a band member who had no say in the material recorded by the Rolling Stones, induced in Brian feelings of resentful exclusion. He was angry that Jagger and Richards had dispensed with the group's blues roots in order to record commercial songs designed for the charts.

But central to my thesis is the belief that Brian Jones, no less than Oscar Wilde, was made the victim of public persecution. Wilde's manner of dress, his bitingly irreverent aphorisms, his extravagant love of pleasure, his belief that the artist was outside moral conventions, and above all his affiliation to a gay ethos enraged the conformist middle classes. The temerity Wilde displayed in acts of social defiance incited the repressed status quo to systematised vengeance. Wilde was victimised by a mob who lacked honesty in their sexual relations, and who were straitjacketed into non-confrontation with their inner demons. The pack, who included the judiciary responsible for Wilde's conviction, were only too well aware of the defendant's sensitivity. Their brutish exercise in moral indignation was to lead to Wilde's death in Paris three years after his release from prison. Oscar was broken by two years hard labour, and during his imprisonment incurred the ear injury, which left unattended was to contribute to the meningitis from which he died in 1900. In sentencing Wilde to hard labour, Mr. Justice Wills effectively signed Oscar's death certificate. In his summing up, Mr. Justice Wills in addressing Wilde and Alfred Taylor, was to state: "It is no use for me to address you. People who can do these things must be dead to all sense of shame, and one cannot hope to produce any effect upon them. It is the worst case I have ever tried."

Wilde and Taylor were not permitted the sort of psychiatric evidence which was to save Brian Jones from being twice imprisoned for being in possession of illegal drugs. The psychiatric plea in Brian's case was that imprisonment could result in the defendant committing suicide, and the report prepared by an independent psychiatrist, Walter Neustatter, was instrumental to Jones's sentence being set aside on three years' probation and a £1,000 fine plus continued medical treatment.

It's interesting for the purposes of our study of Brian as decadent victim to quote some of Dr. Neustatter's assessments of Brian's psychological state at the time. "Mr. Jones's sexual problems," wrote Neustatter, "are closely inter-related to his difficulties of aggression; that is, he experiences very intense anxiety surrounding phallic and sadistic sexuality because of the implicit aggressive striving. However, these phallic strivings are also in conflict with his gross passive dependency needs. The conflict prevents any mature heterosexual adjustment, indeed, he withdraws from any genuine heterosexual involvement ...He vacillates between a passive, dependent child with a confused image of an adult on the one hand, and an idol of pop culture on the other."

Neustatter chooses to focus on Brian's conflicts surrounding sexual identity, as directly pertinent to his subject's outbreaks of violence, potential for psychotic breakdown, and general crisis over gender. Frequent references to Brian's inability to foster heterosexual commitments suggests that the musician may have been troubled by an attraction to homosexual relations. Being gay wasn't something you made public in the sixties. Because they emulated the appearance of girls, the general public lived with the erroneous preconception that the Rolling Stones were making an outwardly political gay statement. Their long-haired, faggoty effeminacy shocked even the cool. A decade later Lou Reed was to provide the anthem for men who dressed as women with his vampishly drawled excursion into transvestite lyrics, "Walk On The Wild Side".

Brian Jones had stood to receive a six month sentence for possession of cannabis and using his home for the consumption of unlawful substances. According to sources around Brian at the time, it was thought that someone in the Stones's organization had deliberately leaked information to the police about his consumption of illegal drugs. Brian was busted on 10 May 1967 by a contingent of ten members of the Scotland Yard Drug Squad, whose diligent autopsy of the flat resulted in their unearthing fifty grains of cannabis. Almost like a vignette extracted from a *fin de siècle* novel, Brian's only companion in the flat at the time was Prince Stanislaus Klossowski De Rola Baron De Watterville. The scene inside Brian's flat at Courtfield Road provided an equally decadent cameo. The residue of an all-night party littered the floor, unsleeved albums were piled up haphazardly, as were bottles, unwashed glasses and crowded ashtrays. Brian, dressed in a gold silk kimono, had only recently got up in the late afternoon. It seemed a disquieting coincidence that Brian was raided on the very day that Mick Jagger and Keith Richards were appearing in Chichester Magistrates' Court at a preliminary hearing for their own bust at Redlands.

The authorities, fed by a vindictive media, had clearly decided to break the Rolling Stones as an example to a libertine sixties youth culture. Although eventually given suspended sentences, both Jagger and Richards in the course of waiting for their appeals to be heard were incarcerated, respectively, in Brixton Prison and Wormwood Scrubs. Jagger's only offence was to have been found in possession of four amphetamine tablets acquired in Italy, and endorsed by his doctor, although only on a verbal basis via the telephone. Richards was charged with allowing his premises to be used for the smoking of cannabis. In a trial so prejudiced that it finds an interface with the Wilde travesty, Jagger was sentenced to three months in prison and Richards to a year, before their sentences were commuted by appeal.

Brian, who was arrested by Detective Sergeant Norman Pilcher, subsequently discharged from the Force in 1973, was made to endure a night in Wormwood Scrubs, while prisoners in adjoining cells howled execrations at him for his feminine appearance. The collective pack bared its fangs in readiness to make Brian its sacrificial victim.

Released the following day, Brian arrived at the Marlborough Street Magistrates Court in his silver Rolls Royce, and as a result of the hearing was remanded on £250 bail, and the case adjourned until 2nd June. Unfortunately, the pressure of events surrounding his arrest triggered in Brian a spiralling persecution mania accompanied by full blown paranoia. He was beginning to nervously disintegrate, and convinced that he was under constant police surveillance, he began to move from one address to another, only to find that the omnipresent stalker lived in his head. Brian's fragile neurology teetered on the edge of psychotic breakdown. Almost to affirm his role as desecrated outlaw, he increased the extravagance of his costume, highlighting his jackets with costume jewellery, and dressing in plum-coloured and maroon women's hats.

Having sensed Brian's easy breakability and his dissolute state of mind, the authorities began to systematically scare his fragmented person. Brian's immediate circle of friends tell of how ambulances and police cars began to call at Courtfield Road, sirens wailing, supposedly having responded to emergency calls that the musician had overdosed in his flat. The use of this psychologically menacing subliminal implant on Brian undermined the last of his confidence. Threatened by his increasingly dysfunctional behaviour with losing his place in the band, and a prey to paid informers within the Stones's organization, Brian began to fall apart.

No sooner had Brian moved to a new flat at 17, Chesham Street in Belgravia, than he was once again visited by the redoubtably ebullient Detective Sergeant Norman Pilcher, this time in connection with a murder investigation. The victim, who was unknown to Brian, was alleged to have been a frequent visitor to the same circuit of clubs. This tenuous linking of two disparate lives served no other purpose than to apply unmediated pressure to the nerve-shot musician. It was at this time that stickers began to appear all over the West End declaring "The Ritual Sacrifice Of Brian Jones", and "Justice For Brian". They mushroomed at night on the expensive facades of buildings in Chelsea and Belgravia.

The hunt to bring Oscar Wilde to ground had been similarly staged. The Marquess of Queensberry had employed his own undercover agents to liaise with the police, in the same way as subterfugal members of the Stones's organization appear to have fed inside information about Brian to the Scotland Yard Drug Squad. Brian was the intelligent member of the Stones, and public hostility towards the latter as purveyors of youth corruption, had the police target Brian as culpable for the radical social changes ushered in by rock music. Brian's sophisticated decadence was in the minds of the authorities a dynamic to be silenced by the weapon of public humiliation.

It was on an autumn night in October 1967, that Brian's blue Rolls Royce was being driven along the Embankment by his chauffeur, Brian Palastanga. Flashed down by the police, who had evidently been informed that Brian had exchanged his ostentatiously ethereal Rolls Royce Silver Cloud for a less conspicuous blue model, both men were frisked and the car's interior methodically searched. The river's fluent obsidian surface reflected lights as an eerie backdrop to the search. Brian's cobalt limousine presented a minor blockage to the arterial flow of traffic heading West and South. His driver was sufficiently quick-thinking to deposit a number of acid tabs wrapped in silver paper beneath his tongue.

After the white, shark-like patrol car had taken off back into the night, Brian made a direct run for the river wall, and screamed that he was going to jump into the Thames. His pink-suited figure balanced a moment on the edge, preparatory to lift-off, before Palastanga grappled him backwards to safety, and then drove him straight to the Priory clinic.

But Brian's problems with the law continued to escalate with dizzying rapidity. In March, 1968, he was to return home to Chesham Street to find his front door had been broken down by a police contingent headed by Detective Sergeant Pilcher, who proceeded to search the apartment. Early in the morning of 20th May, Brian was busted for the second time. Once again, the ominously persistent reverberation of blows to his door awoke a terrified Brian. Once inside, the police produced a ball of blue wool containing a piece of cannabis, an item in no way associated with Brian, the contents of the flat being mostly the property of the actress from whom Brian was renting. Brian was taken to Chelsea police station and formally charged with the unlawful possession of drugs. The arrest was once again the savage persecution of an individual who may have experimented with drugs in private; but who had no interest in dealing or making public his recreation. Fleet Street had been anticipating the arrest for weeks, and were ready with their story before charges were brought.

Eight years later in an interview with *Crawdaddy*, Jagger had this to say of his former colleague's prosecution: "Brian was so sensitive, that was what was so unfair about it, getting busted. It really brought him down. Brian came close to doing six months... He was followed at the time, but we all were. It was a systematic campaign of harassment which brought Brian down and destroyed the musical side of him as well."

It presumably wasn't the drugs, per se, which caused the authorities such vindictive consternation. It was more the altered states of consciousness with which they are associated. Capitalist ideologies function by the manipulative means of keeping the collective immersed in real time. The sixties as a decade were threatened by a youth culture who were discovering the inexhaustible riches of inner space, pacifism by way of the hippies and flower people, unity of gender as an expression of fashion, yoga and meditation through the adoption of Eastern religious practices, and most importantly the freedom to be an individual as it was defined by a youthful pop culture.

The politics of imagination, and the hallucinogenic drugs used in the sixties as part of the drive towards a visionary quest, have always incited material opposition. Western materialism considers decadent those whose preoccupations are with inner events. Being, as opposed to doing, is considered non-contributive to the financial index. A society raised on the legitimized atrocities of two world wars proved manifestly hostile to a sixties generation intent on wearing floral shirts, and re-conditioning gender along the unifying lines of androgyny. Men like Brian Jones were considered to be sissy or sassy, and were viewed as contributing to the degeneracy of masculinity. A retroactive male front resisted the cultural innovations brought in by the publication of Allen Ginsberg's *Howl*, Jack Kerouac's *On The Road*, and the novels of the prototypical faggot junkie, William Burroughs, whose books like *Naked Lunch* explored every deviance of the homosexual and pharmaceutical underworld. It was William Blake, himself rejected by his eighteenth-century contemporaries, who wrote in his *Proverbs Of Hell*: "The road of excess leads to the palace of wisdom." In the same set of proverbs included in *The Marriage Of Heaven And Hell*, Blake emphasised, "He whose face gives no light, shall never become a star." Blake's work found little audience until it was assimilated by the thrust of twentieth-century psychology, and through that medium integrated into a revisioning of poetics.

Brian Jones was an unconscious disciple of Blake's. He more than anyone in the sixties was responsible for the renaissance of the androgyne, both in terms of the spiritual and physical aspect of a powerful archetype. DS Pilcher would have been unaware of Blake's dictum: "Prisons are built with stones of Law, Brothels with bricks of Religion." Brian represented the paradoxical reversion of convention, in the way that Blake deconstructed moral hypocrisy by insighting the holiness of its opposite states. Brian Jones was ritually sacrificed by those who feared the consequences of psychological individuation, and who were resolutely fixed into the idea of uncompromising masculinity. He was murdered not by one hand, but by many, and those who were responsible for his death maintained that they were upholding the law. Oscar Wilde's downfall was brought about by the same punitive mentality. Both men are remembered for their genius, while their detractors are consigned to oblivion.

Brian dances across the pages of this book with a particular shake of his blond hair. It is my intention to follow his steps, and so recreate moments of his life as an unsurpassable decadent.

ONE: **REBEL GENES AND SLIDE GENIUS**

"Brian was probably the most conceited-looking person I have ever met. But he was also one of the most compelling musicians ever on stage."

—Ray Davies

There's a pattern which establishes itself with biographies, in that the first written invariably serves as the referential blueprint for all subsequent undertakings. In this respect, Mandy Aftel's *Death Of A Rolling Stone* (1982), templates the Brian Jones story, and with the exception of later authors naming Frank Thorogood, and two unnamed accomplices as Brian's murderers, there has been little variation in the facts assembled to describe Brian's tragically short life. We tend to accentuate the dysfunctional aspects of Brian's sensibility, and forget that these were the mental confusions of a young man, who granted a longer life may well have passed through what Blake chose to call mental states. Brian had little time in which to apply psychological revision to his naturally paranoid state; and lived immediately and often chaotically at the centre of a decade devoted to cultural revolution. As a person he lacked the methods of psychic self-defence necessary to cope with stardom. The Rolling Stones, like most sixties bands, had started out with no preconceived belief in their permanence. Following in the wake of the unprecedented teenage hysteria attendant on Elvis Presley's American concerts in the late fifties, and those of the Beatles in the opening years of the sixties, the Stones attracted a similar, but rougher response to their rawly impassioned concerts. They were in danger of their lives as insurgently aggressive crowds fought with police stationed in lines to protect the band. Brian was so terrified of the ebullient maelstrom of fans who attended the Stones's every performance, that he would have to be carried into the venue on a friend's or minder's shoulders. Like all hypersensitive paranoids he was attracted to the prospects of stardom, but deeply disquieted by the inroads it made on his privacy. His psyche windowed the unnaturally turbulent changes of the times in which he lived.

Brian was born on 28 February 1942, in Cheltenham, Gloucestershire, the son of Louise, a local piano teacher, and Lewis, an aeronautical engineer with one of Cheltenham's biggest employers, Dowtyd Co. Brian's blond hair and green eyes distinguished him as a sensitive and unconventional child, and a twist of his inveterate rebelliousness was manifest from the earliest of ages. The kink in Brian's behavioural moods was established, while still a child, and although he excelled in music and English at Dean Close Grammar School, Brian rebelled against having to wear an uninspired uniform. At home, he would risk setting fire to his Airfix model planes, and bask in the glory of his pyrotechnical risk. Gifted with an IQ of 135, Brian gravitated to music as his principal study, was taught to read music by his mother, and as a child graduated in stages from the piano to the recorder to the clarinet. Immediately gifted with whatever instrument came to hand, Brian was already a classical deconstructionist, and saw jazz as the modality best suited to his unorthodox musical experimentation. Brian's virtue as a member of the Rolling Stones was to comprise the extraordinary facility with which he introduced instruments like sitar, dulcimer, harpsichord, marimbas and mellotron into a pop format, and something of his later genius was already evident in his years at Dean Close Grammar School.

By his teen years, Brian was recognised at Cheltenham Grammar School as "an intelligent rebel", and as a pupil whose discriminating faculties led him first to question authority, and later to suffer the consequences of opposing it. He came into conflict with the authorities by refusing to wear the standard straw boater, something accepted as *de rigueur* in that draconian regime, and by leading an intramural revolt against the prefects. It was truculent behaviour on his part that had him suspended from school, much to the mortification of his father. Brian's father seems to have played the role of an admonitory incubus to his son, and to have been unnecessarily officious in enquiring after his behaviour at school. It was accepted practice amongst fifties parents that they monitored a child's education, and in this respect Brian's father was probably guilty of being over-assiduous in tracking his son's progress at school. To a sensitive teenager like Brian, parental interference was tantamount to persecution. On a psychological level it amplified his innate feelings of guilt.

Brian was also in trouble at school for growing his blond-orange hair to his collar, an insubordinate act which was considered outrageous in the fifties. Not since the foppish aesthetes of Wilde's generation had men worn their hair long, and Brian's style right from the start emulated a woman's hairdo. Brian's hyperactive sensibility suffered from the endemic teenage malaise of boredom. With his desires repressed by domestic and grammar school conformism, he turned inward to feed his musical aspirations. Even before he was expelled from school for making an off-limits pupil at the select Girls' Grammar pregnant, Brian was inhabiting coffee bars in town, and developing exceptional skills as a guitarist, pianist and saxophonist.

There's something about Brian' premature sexual licentiousness which speaks of desperation. Making the girl pregnant may have been a way of convincing himself of his heterosexuality, as well as comprising an act of moral defiance. The girl refused to have an abortion, and the incident became a local scandal. It was as though Brian had thrown a boulder into a serene pool. Even his schoolfriends shunned him for his aberrant behaviour. In his mind he came to identify with the Beats – the generation of writers and musicians who influenced by Allen Ginsberg and Jack Kerouac were laying the foundations for what was to become the permissive sixties. Brian's psychic attunement, no matter his upbringing in provincial Cheltenham, was to the apocalyptic cultural changes in which as a musician and image-leader he was to play so vital a part. It was Blake who wrote: "What is now proved was once only imagined". Brian Jones as a musician was a catalyst for some of the fulfilments of Blakean prophecy which were realised in the triggered adrenaline-rush of social costume changes which characterised sixties culture. Inspired creative sensibilities are often made flesh with the purpose of intersecting with a particular moment in time. Brian was an instance of youthful genius. Like Arthur Rimbaud, the child-poet who revolutionised not only poetry, but the way we perceive the universe, Brian burnt himself out young. His early flash fulminated in his eyes, and he was dead before he could properly evaluate the significance of his work.

But back in Cheltenham in 1960, Brian occupied himself with hanging out in the then fashionable world of coffee bars. He had spent the summer of 1959 hitching through Scandinavia, until on the brink of starvation, he had been forced to return home. Again, there's the analogy with Arthur Rimbaud, who in his early teens would run away from his local Charlesville, and invariably head in the direction of Paris. Brian, who also had begun to sit in with various jazz combos, made similar journeys to London, and was evidently in search of a music which he had still to formulate. The idea was there, and it was part of his restlessness, but the moment had not yet arrived for his creative expression to find form.

There is the distinct possibility that during his itinerant interlude to Scandinavia and Germany, Brian had to sell his body to live, and Pat Andrews, the girlfriend he was to meet on his return to Cheltenham, has intimated at the possibility by saying, "It's not that Brian wouldn't have been open to an experience like that. But it was the circumstances. It just wasn't right."

On his return to Cheltenham, Brian took refuge in coffee bars with names like the Patio, the Aztec, the El Flam and, most popular of all, the Barbecue/Waikiki in Queen's Circus. He would earn subsistence money playing with a local jazz band the Cheltone Six, but was largely reliant on his parents for financial support. At this stage of his life Brian was to find himself confronted by the paradoxical dilemma applicable to most creative sensibilities, which is the inherent irreconcilability of time and money. It is rare that we experience both, and those with an inner disposition invariably need time in which to bring their work to some form of creative realisation. But money is necessary too, and Brian found himself resorting to taking jobs as a coalman and as a factory worker in order to finance a time of waiting for his musical aspirations to ring true.

It was at the Aztec, that Jones met and became involved with the sixteen-year old Patricia Andrews, who at the time was working in the local Boots. Andrews was attracted to Brian's innate shyness, his superior intelligence, his willingness to listen in conversation, his dynamic energies, and of course the eloquent passion with which he would speak about music.

Brian's academic record of nine GCE O levels and two A level passes was to secure him a short-lived job with the architects' department of the Gloucestershire County Council. He showed genuine merit in this capacity, but his obsession was with playing music, and once again he was to drift away from a half-formed attempt to meet the criteria imposed by the conditions of regular employment.

Brian was sustained in this period of inchoate direction by his friendship with Richard Hattrell, and the two friends were to end up sharing a tiny flat at 73 Prestbury Road in Cheltenham's bohemian sector. By this time, early in 1961, Brian had formed a successful rock'n'roll instrumental combo called The Ramrods. He clearly knew inwardly that his resolve to fingerprint contemporary music with the innovative sounds that he was hearing on record in the playing of artists like Muddy Waters, would in time grow to be a reality. It is when the revolutionary and creative aspects of the individual marry that the artist is born. Certainly his violent mood oscillations were already evident in his behaviour, as was the continuance of Brian's sexual irresponsibility, something marked by his making Pat Andrews pregnant. Brian was, by his mid-twenties, to find himself impotent, the impairment arising from psychological issues, and his early need to prove his masculinity seems to speak of a desperate compulsion on his part to find some place in the system of orthodox relations. Brian named his son, Mark, but had no intentions of marrying, or of even nominally supporting mother and child. His personality seems to have dissociated from practical responsibilities, which is often the way with the creative temperament. The artistic side of him could find little or no purchase on reality.

This psychological rift in Brian was a dichotomy that had some of his contemporaries refer to him as schizoid. While Brian wasn't clinically schizophrenic, the dissociative aspects of his personality were also much later to inform his recklessly extravagant spending. As a successful musician he would on impulse make ludicrously superfluous purchases, like the acquisition of a London bus, or raid antique markets with a compulsion to possess whatever pleased his eye. There was something of the mad characteristics of Ludwig II of Bavaria, about Brian, and Ludwig's architectural extravaganzas, his love of young men, and his almost child-like preoccupation with a blue subterranean grotto, would have found a compatible interface with Brian Jones's love of the eccentrically bizarre.

Brian and Cheltenham simply weren't compatible in terms of

allowing the young musician the facilities with which to realise his dreams. Visits to the town by the Chris Barber jazz band, and Brian's blues hero Alexis Korner, only increased his resolve to establish himself in London, where there was an active jazz and blues scene. For years, Brian had been recording all he could of Alexis's music, as it was broadcast on the radio, and Korner's coming to play at the Cheltenham Town Hall created for the young Brian a chance to meet and talk with his blues apotheosis. A friendship was formed from the start, and Alexis was to invite his young protegé to visit and stay with him in London. Describing his first meeting with Brian, Alexis was to remember him as: "This pent-up ball of obsessive energy, talking away to the dozen in an incredibly intense manner".

Brian's loquaciousness was hardly surprising in view of the blues comprising a secret vocabulary amongst players. Even methods of playing were concealed by slide guitarists, and Brian's own tutorials comprised incessant hours of listening to records by Elmore James. Brian's compulsive quest for a homemade slide-bar ended in his salvaging a bit of utilizable piping from a plumbers' yard, and cutting it to two inches as a perfect fit for his finger. Increasingly adept at coaxing emotion from his guitar, Brian sniffed that London was to be his creative locus, and began to make frequent visits to the capital to hear Alexis Korner and his Blues Incorporated play at the Ealing Jazz Club. Basing himself in a flat in Notting Hill Gate, impecunious but dandified in a flamboyant Italian box-jacket and winklepicker shoes, Brian began sitting in at the Wooden Bridge Hotel, Guildford, with a scratch band called Rhode Island Red and the Roosters. Brian's determination to succeed as an innovative blues musician took precedence over every other aspect of his life. This singular resolve, and the corresponding ruthlessness he employed in setting about realising his ideal, was to place an unnatural strain on his relationship with the supportive Pat Andrews. Brian's life is best described in terms of a meteoric shooting star which burnt too bright to sustain its orbit.

It was as at the Wooden Bridge Hotel that Brian first made the acquaintance of Paul Pond, later to become Paul Jones, the vocalist with Manfred Mann. It was while Jones was performing with Pond at the Ealing Club on 7 April, 1962, that he came to the attention of Mick Jagger and Keith Richards. Jagger had already performed occasional sets as a second-string vocalist for Alexis Korner's band, and like Brian he nurtured an instinctual love of black Chicago blues artists like Chuck Berry, Bo Diddley and Muddy Waters.

Brian's guitar playing that night on a Gibson with its pearl-inlaid neck was reputedly awesome. He evoked a sensitively mournful eloquence with his frets, and his inspired musicianship apart, was separated from the other players by virtue of his appearance. Dressed in a dark blue Italian suit, and wearing a white tab-collar shirt with an obligatory black knitted tie, he was the embodiment of the sartorial prototype of early sixties fashion. The raffish, chunky-cardiganed audience, which included Jagger and Richards, looked up to Brian as a forerunner of the youth culture about to burn a trail across the impending decade. Brian's style was already synonymous with decadence in that he clearly lived for his art and nothing else. Dick Taylor, a friend of Jagger and Richards, and later to be a member of the Pretty Things, remembered the fixating experience of first seeing and hearing Brian, as such: "I first saw Brian when he and Paul Jones were announced on stage by Alexis that night at Ealing. Brian sat down and began playing slide guitar extremely well. I mean real riveting stuff. Both of them were wearing shades... And Brian, he was doing a 'Robert Johnson', like he would turn his back on the audience and all that. Real calm, you know..."

Brian was more than a stage natural and a cool performer shielded by the mystique that shades provide. He was also the intransigent, bisexual *zeitgeist* of a generation beginning to scent its explosive potential. In this respect, Brian Jones was a decade in advance of David Bowie's androgynous revelations through the persona of Ziggy Stardust, only Brian was too close to his age for his impacted relevance as a bisexual icon to be assimilated. Brian's contributions to gay culture were suppressed by a management intent on marketing the Rolling Stones as a product of subversive machismo, and all of his subsequent biographers, excepting Nicholas Fitzgerald, have made little issue of Brian's sexual relations with men. This almost unilateral assumption of Brian's profligate heterosexuality has done much to limit an understanding of the sassier aspects of his genius. I would go so far as to say that it was the gay components of Brian's complex gender orientation which accounted for his creative panache as a musician, and as a fashion leader to his generation.

At the time of their first meeting with Brian, Jagger was a student at the London School of Economics and Keith Richards was attending Sidcup Art School. Encouraged by their shared love of rhythm and blues, and with the addition of Ian Stewart on piano,

Dick Taylor on bass and Mick Avory drums, Brian named the band the Rolling Stones after a favourite Muddy Waters song – "Rollin' Stone Blues". The band made a frenzied and controversial debut at London's Marquee club, the performance setting a riotous blueprint for later concerts by an invasion of Mod enthusiasts who turned violently on the audience. The Rolling Stones had begun as they were to continue, on a note of hectic insurrection inspired by the double presence of Jagger and Jones's on-stage antics.

Soon after their Marquee debut, the Rolling Stones started to pick up dates at the Ealing Club and the Oxford Street Club. As a sign of the aspiring bohemianism that sealed their camaraderie, Brian together with Jagger and Richards moved into a semi-derelict two room flat at number 102 Edith Grove, in London's fashionable Chelsea, SW10 district. In a rat-infested, unheated apartment, and often without money to feed the electric metre, Brian and Keith Richards studied the infrastructure of blues guitar by listening to records by Jimmy Reed and Muddy Waters. Recollecting their beginnings from the standpoint of fame, Brian was to remember: "We wondered if we were doing the right thing by not getting into worthwhile jobs and forgetting all about this music bit... Suppose we failed. Suppose we went on not doing much, just soaking up music, for a whole year. That would be the limit, we reckoned. If we flopped – would it matter? At least we'd have tried..."

Any durable creative endeavour evolves from a germinating period of silence. It is in the preparatory time away from the world that ideas take shape and form the basis of future achievements. Brian shoplifted, as the painter Francis Bacon had done before him, and supplemented his poverty with occasional earnings. The cold was the worst adversary, and the brilliant winter freeze crept into the rooms at Edith Grove like an insidiously glacial cat. Brian would have to stay in bed to keep warm, and played guitar tented in a wrap of blankets. But even in the untenable cold, he maintained the ritual of shampooing his luxuriously fringed blond hair. It would have been easy to concede defeat, but Brian was sustained by the vision of a music which was fomented in his blood. His only direction forward was the one dictated by the music.

Faced with urgent hire purchase repayments on their stage equipment, the Rolling Stones were threatened with premature extinction, and saved only by the fact that Brian worked with ferocious resolve to secure the band an increasing string of low-profile dates. Their sporadic appearances at the prestigious Marquee club were terminated that autumn, when Keith Richards broke his guitar over the head of a derisory Harold Pendleton, the club's owner. The repercussions of Richards' violent authentication that the Rolling Stones had arrived to supersede an older generation was to result in a substantial loss of dates, and to the Stones' bass player, Dick Taylor, deciding to return to his studies at the Royal College of Art. The latter was to be replaced by Bill Wyman, who owned a Vox Phantom bass, together with a bass cabinet, and shortly afterwards the Stones were to benefit from the addition of a new drummer in the person of Charlie Watts.

It was now January 1963, and the Rolling Stones had formed a musical unit which would remain unchanged until Brian's death in 1969. The self-improvised musical education that Jones and Richards had undertaken at Edith Grove was about to be translated into the primitive blues-pop attack which characterised the Stones's early sound. Reflecting on their formative virtuoso styles, Keith Richards has said: "I found myself very much with Brian, playing music, listening to records over and over again trying to figure it all out, how it's actually played, for hours and hours every day. At this point Brian was a phenomenal guitarist. He always had to work at it because he never did develop a style particularly of his own. He used to get turned on by listening."

Brian had also begun to experiment with harmonica, and through his friendship with Cyril Davies, he learnt the latter's technique of bending and flattening notes. He developed an idiosyncratic manner of playing, which owed much to the hanging fire method adopted by Jimmy Reed. Brian's characteristic restlessness had him quickly discard new sounds, and with an almost reckless perversity he would as the decade deepened augment his musicianship by playing a bewilderingly diverse repertoire of increasingly exotic instruments. He mastered nothing, but succeeded in extracting eloquent colouring from whatever he played. His approach to an instrument was prompted by intuitive understanding of the sound required. Brian's role as a maverick musical colourist came by way of establishing an instinctive discourse with the tool at his disposal. Endowed with an almost mediumistic faculty of apprehending a sound before he was able to play it, Brian might be considered as an instrumental clairvoyant.

Back in London, in January 1963, the Stones started out the

year by playing at the Flamingo Club in Soho. Coming to the attention of Glyn Johns, senior engineer at I.B.C. Recording Studio, the band – who were not yet signed to a label – were invited to I.B.C. Studio to record five rhythm and blues covers. With Jagger's voice considered suspectly weak by all present, the band cut "Diddley Daddy", "Road Runner", "Bright Lights, Big City", "I Want To Be Loved", and "Honey, What's Wrong?". The choice of songs was made by Brian, who played harmonica and guitar on all tracks, in addition to singing back-up vocals. The overtly raw untutored, wonkily offbeat rhythm and blues texture established by the Stones in their first session left Glyn Johns amazed at the punkish alacrity with which they executed numbers. Their music sounded un-categorically modern to the engineer's ear, and he felt unnerved by their fluently precocious attitude. Brian was evidently the leader of the raffish ensemble, and it was he who conferred with Johns on points of technique contributing to the band's required sound.

The band's frustration at having their demo tape rejected by both EMI and Decca was no deterrent to their growing popularity on the club circuit. Due once again to Brian's coercive faculties, and his friendship with a London club promoter called Giorgio Gomelski, the Stones began to get bookings at the Crawdaddy club situated in the back room of the Station Hotel in Richmond. Mods, Rockers, Beatniks and Teddy Boys commingled in queues outside the club, the whole assembled youth culture beginning to scent the animalistic qualities of the new music engendered by the Rolling Stones. The band were rightly billed as "The Thrilling Stones". A local paper, *The Richmond And Twickenham Times*, gave the Stones their first review coverage, and complimented the band by noting: "The deep, earthy sound is typical of the best R&B, and gives all who hear it an irresistible urge to stand up and move".

It was at the Crawdaddy club that Andrew Oldham, who had been doing peripheral publicity for the Beatles, first saw the Rolling Stones deliver a high-octane charged R&B set, infused with the band's idiosyncratically edgy colouring. Brian's movements with the tambourine were electrifying, and Jagger's anorexically-wired sexuality lit a volatile fuse in the audience. Oldham, together with a booking agent called Eric Easton, with whom he shared an office at Randor House, Regent Street, were blown away by the band's impacted magnetism. Dressed now in high tab-collar shirts and leather waistcoats, the Rolling Stones both looked and sounded like insurgently upcoming revolutionaries.

Alexis Korner has recalled Brian's seminal influence as a charismatically subversive performer in the Stones's chaotic early concerts. "In terms of feeling," Alexis recollected, "Brian was vitally important to the Stones because he had more edge to him than any of the others. And he was the nasty one. I mean the whole nasty image of the Stones really started with Brian, not Mick. Because Brian was a bitch." Extending the metaphor of Brian's arrogant bitchiness, when in discourse with an audience, Alexis continued: "You'd see him dancing forward with a tambourine and snapping it in your face and sticking his tongue out at you. In a nasty way. Not a school-boyish way. And then he'd move back before you actually took a punch at him."

Brian's initial upfront extroversion as a performer was to disappear in proportion to Jagger's vampirical upstaging of his blond colleague's mannerisms. By 1964–65 Brian's magnetism was created largely by his effeminate posturing, and by his visual attraction to audiences on the level of being a narcissistic poseur. Brian was progressively forced to compensate for his passive role in the group by drawing attention to himself through the extraordinary opulence of his feminine dress.

Brian, who was now in the process of leaving Pat Andrews, in order to begin still another callous relationship, this time with Linda Lawrence, signed a three year management contract with the enthusiastic Oldham and Easton on 1st May, 1963. Brian signed on behalf of all members of the Rolling Stones, none of whom were consulted, but all of whom were to quickly benefit from Oldham's astute managerial vitality in securing the band a recording contract with Decca.

Brian's offensive front on stage was of course an adopted persona, and his cultivated sensibility was to react with innate disrelish to Oldham's image of the group as a bunch of moronic renegades. In contradistinction to the more domestic-friendly image employed by the Beatles as a means to securing international fame, Oldham played up the notion of the Rolling Stones as being hostile to society. His tabloid propagations like, "Would You Let Your Daughter Marry A Rolling Stone?" put the group into immediate contention with the public. It was a position that Brian was often at pains to correct by pointing out that contrary to media opinion he did wash, and more importantly took meticulous care of his expensive appearance.

Right from those early days, an air of competitiveness existed in the Stones camp and Jagger and Richards found themselves forming a triumvirate with Oldham, to the exclusion of the hypersensitive Brian. Richards has reflected: "There was always this incredible conflict between Brian, Mick and myself. It was imbalanced in one way or another. There was something between us that didn't quite make it somewhere. Maybe it's in the stars. Brian was a Pisces, I'm a Sagittarius, and Mick's a Leo. Maybe those three can't ever completely connect all together at the same time for very long."

Brian's system was already under acute nervous strain, and symptomatic of his exhaustion, and possibly psychosomatically induced, were complaints like ear infections, back problems, nervous stomach, and a variety of illnesses associated with his anxious temperament. Although Brian assiduously courted fame and recognition, the pressures attendant on being a pop star were to make massive inroads on his always precarious health. It would be true to say that throughout his career with the Rolling Stones Brian functioned in the impaired state of increasingly deleterious nervous exhaustion. He would disappear without notification into health clinics, or would dematerialise and be uncontactable by his management. Brian conformed to the narcissistic archetype, his compulsion was to explore his intrinsic pathology to the exclusion of reality. In this respect, it is not without profound significance that he, like Narcissus, should die by drowning.

Part of the tragedy for Brian was that his particular spectrum of nervous suffering met with no sympathetic ear within the Stones's obtusely hardened organisation. There is a feeling that if Brian had been surrounded by a more culturally sophisticated circle, then his difficulties would have been shared, and at least tolerated. As it was, he found himself brutally dismissed as a hypochondriac, and was considered to be a health liability by an avaricious management. Brian's way of dealing with the uncomfortable situation was to degenerately self-destruct. On an emotional level he took refuge with female look-alikes, who provided him with the narcissistic mirror-image of his anima. In reality he was surrounded by semi-criminal minders employed by the Stones's office, who stole from him, and took a perverse delight in accelerating his mercurial process of self-destruction.

For the first three years of the Oldham-Easton managerial

partnership, Brian found a more sympathetic ear in Easton, and by the time the latter was voted out in 1966, Brian's position within the band was wholly untenable. And the more paranoid Brian became, the less he was able to work.

The Rolling Stones's first single "Come On" was released on the Decca label in England on 7 June, 1963, and in September of the same year the band undertook their first English tour, an attraction which also featured Bo Diddley and the Everly Brothers. "Come On" proved to be a minor hit, but the song disappointingly failed to generate the distinctive energies that the Stones were creating live. The hot, androgynous flash of their stage volatility was absent from their studio sound, a weakness repeated on their second, slightly more successful single, "I Wanna Be Your Man". Ironically, their second single's possible bisexual orientation – Jagger could have been addressing men rather than women – was lost on a media intent on framing the Stones as morally depraved outlaws. It wasn't until January 1964, by which time the Rolling Stones had become the most popular live act in the country, that they recorded a single equal to their musical talents. The song was of course the Buddy Holly number "Not Fade Away", which Brian typically punctuated with ululating harmonica bursts. Recorded at night in Regent Sound, the Stones had never sounded so unmatchably confident in their youthful arrogance. The sneer in Jagger's voice, and his contemptuous streetwise delivery of the lyrics, had him appear as a diffident advocate of promiscuity.

"Not Fade Away" made it to No. 2 in the British charts, confirming that the Rolling Stones had arrived, no matter the hostility directed at their long hair and seemingly outrageous lifestyles. The group not only represented a new expression of music in the form of an energised conflation of R&B and bruised pop modalities, but through their looks up-ended all preconceptions of gender standards. By the time the band appeared on Arthur Haynes's television show to deliver a poignant, slouchily phrased, acoustic rendition of "You Better Move On", the eyebrow-level fringes sported by Jones and Jagger were sufficient to have the switchboard jammed with irate complaints. Television shows which had hosted the Rolling Stones were issued with hate mail, and the President of the National Federation of Hairdressers directed his acrimony at Brian's blond page-boy cut by declaring: "The Rolling Stones are the worst. One of them looks as though he has got a feather duster on his head".

With Brian living part of the time at Linda Lawrence's Windsor home, the Rolling Stones, who had released their first instantly chart-topping LP on 26 April 1964, began the incessant and physically debilitating touring that was to mark the next three years of their meteoric trajectory to fame. There were riots everywhere they played, and audience dementia seriously threatened the band's mortality. Brian's clothes would be shredded from his body should he risk coming to the lip of the stage, and police protection was a necessary part of security at every venue. Brian's cavalier propensity for velvet-collared suits, striped blazers, white shoes, lambswool sweaters and a variety of Carnaby Street high collar shirts were in evidence on stage, as he fugitively looked out at the maelstromic horde of hysterical, nubile girls. Often the band would be forced to run for their lives, as the mob invaded the stage.

In 1964, the Rolling Stones undertook their first American tour, and Brian was put into regular panic states by the chaotically invasive dynamic of their fans. The blond hair which he conceived as a sacrosanct fetish was constantly at risk of being brutally uprooted by marauding girls. The more Brian's private space was invaded, the greater the likelihood there was of his doing a paranoid flip. "A lot of the time," Alexis Korner reflected, "Brian didn't know who he was. He was very finely balanced from the nervous point of view, very finely balanced indeed. He was given to 100 percent shifts of reaction in a matter of seconds. It was very obvious he had problems controlling his own head at times. He was intelligent enough to be able to work out certain things to save himself, but without the desire to do them. He was also into that thing which a lot of us are into: when you get into a particularly dangerous path you want to know how far you can survive it. In relationships with others as well as in relationship with himself he had this funny on-and-off balance."

Back in Britain, the Stones's fourth single, the Bobby Womack composition "It's All Over Now", went straight to the top of the charts. The song was recorded at Chess recording studios in Chicago, with the band benefiting from the technological expertise of Chess and the house engineer Ron Malo. The record's success was to be repeated later in the year with the threnodic blues of "Little Red Rooster", a courageously slow-tempo down-mooded song in which the purposely crestfallen vocal is upheld by Brian's virtuosic slide guitar. The latter song, which comprises pure indigenous blues, was to remain Brian's paradigmatic favourite of the singles released by the

Rolling Stones during his tenure with the band. Ominous for Brian, by the close of 1964, was Andrew Oldham's resolve to have Jagger and Richards team off into a songwriting partnership. Brian had been secretly composing for years, but it was his manner to keep his compositions private, as though he feared his poetic lyrics would meet with ridicule. Linda Lawrence has claimed that when Brian was living with her in her parents' home in Windsor, he would sit at the kitchen table half the night, totally concentrated into his nocturnal art of writing lyrics. There was something about Jagger's extrovert monomania, as it was exercised within a creative precinct, which induced feelings of inferiority in Brian. Brian's inspirational space was suffocated in the studio by the now authoritative measures of the songwriting duo, Jagger and Richards.

Encouraged by the example of Lennon and McCartney's songwriting successes with the Beatles, and by the lucrative prospects of self-composition, Jagger and Richards began to compose the infectiously poppy numbers which characterised the Stones's mid-sixties sound. Brian conceived this Oldham-inspired commercial move as essentially undermining the band's musicianship. The notion of the singer/songwriter, as the concept evolved in the sixties, irrespective of talent, has in large done irreparable damage to the lyric side of the equation. Jagger is often an uninspired and forced lyricist, dependent on slurred phrasing to disguise the song's weaknesses. But given his inimitable qualities as a performer, and a contagious riff on which to surf, then his lyrics sound no better or worse than most of his contemporaries. When in 1965, the Rolling Stones went straight to the top of the British charts with the release of their first self-penned single, "The Last Time", for Brian the writing on the wall was alarmingly clear.

The successful pop formula generated by Jagger/Richards was to extend to another five successive chart-topping British singles over the next two years. It was a programme which was to engender the hit singles: "(I Can't Get No) Satisfaction", "Get Off My Cloud", "19th Nervous Breakdown", "Paint It Black", and "Have You Seen Your Mother, Baby, Standing In The Shadows".

Brian naturally felt excluded from the commercial prerogative mandated by his two colleagues. As the founder member of the Rolling Stones he had seen himself reduced to becoming an instrumental colourist, a musician who contributed little more than studio flourishes to other people's songs. The resentment that Brian felt at having his creativity undermined, was directed inwardly, and repressed rage at his reduced status within the band led him not only to be violent to the various women in his life, but brutal to himself by way of self-destructive alcoholism. Jagger's daemonic persona threatened Brian with extinction, as the vocalist became ever more the spokesman and performance pivot around which the group revolved. Brian, who had begun combining alcohol with pharmaceuticals in an attempt to assuage his inner wounds, was thrown into a state of panicked chaos. Marianne Faithfull has recalled the confused turmoil in which Brian endeavoured to compose. Vignetting Brian's life at Courtfield Road, she has drawn attention in *Year One* to incidents involving his frustrated creativity. Faithfull recollects: "Manic scribbling in notebooks followed by pages being ripped out. Then the frantic business with the tapes would start. Recording, erasing, recording, erasing. Reels unspooling all over the floor, the offending tapes being hurled across the room. These were Brian's phantom songs."

After his death, Brian's tapes became a part of disinformation, and one wonders if his random, endlessly self-corrected attempts at writing songs will surface one day in the form of a cache of concealed material. Did Brian's songs accompany him in phaoronic style into his tomb? Faithfull has told us of the musician painting a graveyard mural on the wall behind his bed at Courtfield Road, and perhaps in the unlawful dispersal of his personal effects soon after his death, his working tapes were stolen in the jumble of purloined possessions.

Brian's lifestyle did little to assist his health. As his anxieties over the band's apparent take-over by Jagger and Richards increased, so his addictive smoking grew to proportions of sixty cigarettes a day. Heavy smoking exacerbated his asthma, and it became necessary for him to carry a Ventalin inhaler at all times. He had also begun to rely on alcohol to anaesthetise his shot nerves, and he quickly developed an alarming penchant for whisky, brandy, and the popular sixties spirit mix of Bacardi and Coke. The band's relentless schedule of touring also contributed to inadequate nutrition on Brian's part and, reliant largely on junk food snatched between shows, his body had little chance to detox. The introduction of recreational drugs into Brian's imbalanced neurology was to prove the most potently destructive component in this dangerous cocktail of toxins. By the time of his death in 1969, Brian's liver was manifesting signs of fatty degeneration, and his heart was abnormally enlarged for a man still in his twenties.

In retrospect we ask ourselves, was it the intolerable pressures of being in a hugely successful and controversial band which destroyed Brian, or was his death-drive an ineradicably innate aspect of his psyche? Brian, who had anticipated a career as a popular bluesman, a role which would have been confined to playing to club-size audiences, undoubtedly found himself unable to cope with the ravaging menace instigated by fan hysteria. He was like somebody who had lit a fire, and unable to tolerate the ensuing furnace decided that the only way out was to jump into the raging flames. The black pendant pouches beneath Brian's eyes told a story of nocturnal dissolution. With his eyes continually screened by a defensive fringe of blond hair, so that he appeared almost like a shy girl, Brian's features nonetheless mapped out a narrative of destructively hedonistic nights. In the decadent tradition, Wilde had spent his nights at Kettners, the Alhambra, the St James', and other bars inhabited by rent boys. Brian, who appeared to be permanently dressed in drag, was whisked across London at night in chauffeur-driven cars which took him to a circuit of fashionable clubs, or he was to be found at home, morosely sitting on the edge of an orgiastic party.

Throughout 1965–66, Brian continued to texture the Stones's music with gracefully peacocked flourishes. He became adept at decorative colouring, and his musical palette is nowhere in better evidence than on the seminally innovative *Aftermath* album of 1965. For many fans *Aftermath* represents the Rolling Stones at their most melodic. While the album is simplistically poppy, it also retains undertones of the band's R&B origins, and particularly so in the Jones harmonica-orchestrated number "Goin' Home". On *Aftermath* Brian was to extend his musical acumen to experimenting with harpsichord, dulcimer, sitar, marimbas and even a child's plastic banjo. His sensitive highlighting of basic pop songs with adventurously bizarre instrumentation, was to change the course of sixties pop music, and to impart to *Aftermath* a modernism which has allowed it to survive the decades with distinction.

Brian's instrumental eclecticism has mostly been construed as the dilettante signature of a butterfly maverick. He would pick up an instrument, magic it into co-operation, and then quickly tire of its potential. Of this method, Keith Altham, who interviewed Brian at the time of the *Aftermath* sessions, has written: "It was almost a natural feel he had for picking up instruments and playing them immediately, but he was limited in what he could do. As soon as he found out he could play a few bits and pieces on it, he didn't have the discipline or the concentration to stick at it and take it any further. Just like the latest plaything, pick it up, play it, put it down and forget it, which was a bit like how he was with people."

But all of Brian's exquisite musical sensitivity permeates the songs on *Aftermath*, and nowhere more so than in underlining the Tudor tenor of "Lady Jane", which features his tinkling dulcimer to poignant effect. His use of redemptive marimbas on the sneeringly misogynistic "Under My Thumb", his showcasing harpsichord on the plaintive "I Am Waiting", and his preternaturally spooky harmonica punctuating "Goin' Home", also indicate an inventiveness amounting to quirkily unorthodox genius. It was on "Paint It Black", an immediate No. 1 single culled from the same sessions at RCA Hollywood from 3–12 March 1966, that Brian's sitar proved to be the compelling instrument around which the song hangs. David Dalton, in his book *The Rolling Stones: The First Twenty Years*, has written eloquently of Brian's contribution to "Paint It Black". Dalton writes: "Brian's attack on the sitar was innovative. His playing was more percussive than melodic, sharper and more treble, exploiting its tonal range in a way George Harrison's respectful treatment did not begin to explore. Brian's innovation was to integrate the sitar into the total sound of 'Paint It Black'. He gave the sitar a rock inflection with a shrill, metallic, twangy sound that was closer to an electric guitar than to an exotic stringed instrument."

Reports from the studio sessions for *Aftermath* say that Brian spent much of the time disinterestedly lying on his back on the floor, and was motivated to contribute only in short bursts of unpredictable inspiration. It was his way of protesting at having to play material exclusively written by Jagger and Richards. The case of Brian now being a dispensable appendage to a commercial pop band has been strongly argued, but whether his delegation to the role of ludic prettifier of melodies was responsible for his rapid personal dissolution, is still an open question. From the time of the *Aftermath* sessions, Brian expressed disinterest in playing guitar, claiming either that his fingers hurt, or that he wasn't satisfied with his performance. The perverse strangulation of his considerable talent as a slide guitarist, preferring to silence what would have been a major contribution to the Stones's sound was, of course, another expression of Brian's deeply destructive self-hatred. With the new self-written material being structured round Keith Richards's formative riffs, Brian's way of hitting back was to suppress his own virtuosic guitar genius. The band's mid-sixties records had wandered a long way from Brian's blues pivot, and in the effort to circumvent what he considered to be pop banality, Brian set about texturing the format with the sophisticated complexity of unusual instruments. In this respect, Brian was the catalyst for almost all forms of progressive rock.

Although Brian continued to play guitar on the band's tours, and to contribute some superb playing to 1968's *Beggars Banquet* album, he did so with expressed dissatisfaction. Phil May, the vocalist with the Pretty Things, an intransigent sixties band whose career ran contemporaneous with the Rolling Stones, has expressed his adamant belief that Brian's guitar sound was centrifugal to the band's success. In Phil May's estimate: "Brian was very important to the Stones, incredibly essential. You can see that by the fact that the Stones have never been the same without him... Anyone else up there, and I've nothing against either Mick Taylor or Ron Wood, is just another guitarist. It was something spiritual with Brian. He was a left wing – a spiritual element. You could have cut off Brian's guitar arm and he'd still have had it. Even the problems surrounding him in the band were central to the electricity of the Stones."

It was in 1965 that Brian met Anita Pallenberg, one of the blonde clones to whom he was invariably attracted. Originating from a long line of wealthy Swiss and German artists, Pallenberg's good looks and hauteur had taken her into the world of modelling. The two were to form an intensely vampirical union, their violent domestic conflicts often ending in Brian growing hysterical and resorting to physical violence in the attempt to silence the tempestuous altercation. But together their looks interfaced the archetypal androgyne. Brian discovered his anima in Anita, and Anita her animus in Brian. When Brian moved out of his Fulham mews cottage to the luxurious Courtfield Road apartment, Pallenberg was to move in with him, and for a brief time afford Brian the emotional security that seems always to have been absent from his life. It is unlikely that Brian would ever have found fulfilment in a monogamous relationship with either a woman or man, as his essentially introverted and narcissistic sensibility resisted love. The aesthete self-loves, rather than looks to correlate emotions with others. In this respect Brian's psychological insighting of life was predominantly interiorized. He inhabited a delusional world of paranoid fantasies, and used the felicitous privilege of wealth to buy his way out of practical quandaries. His insecurities were such that while he surrounded himself with an entourage, he allowed nobody access to his inner world.

Some of Brian's inherent gallery of complexes have been related by former girlfriends, most of whom discovered that Brian was sexually dysfunctional. His former French girlfriend, Zouzou, has recounted how Brian's identification with the female would have him telephone hospitals about the idea of undergoing transformative surgery to have his face changed to resemble a woman's. Brian was too complicated and too inhibited to make love to his innumerable conquests. His bisexuality was undoubtedly an inhibitor in heterosexual relations, and alcohol and drugs would have additionally depressed his libidinal appetites. Brian envied women the body he had been denied. His impulse towards psychic identification with the transsexual was a pronounced aspect of his psychological makeup. The surgically consummated transsexual disinherits his parents. His or her original gender as it was parented is rendered inoperative by the individual's election to change sex. Brian's resentment at the manner in which his parents had actively discouraged his musical aspirations, while at the same time denouncing him as a social failure for his refusal to adopt a middle class profession, was at the roots of his desire to recreate his gender. As the sixties progressed so Brian came increasingly to work on the obscuration of his male sexuality.

Marianne Faithfull has written of her youthful experience in having Brian attempt to make love to her at Courtfield Road. "So after several large spliffs," Faithfull writes, "and what I gathered was courtship patter (involving the Flying Scotsman, Mary Wells, William Morris wallpaper and Tantric art), Brian led me up the little staircase to the minstrel's gallery. We lay down on a mattress and he un-buttoned my blouse. But after a bit of groping about, it just fizzled out. He was a wonderfully feeble guy, quite incapable of real sex. And, of course, he was doing a lot of Mandrax, which rendered him even more wobbly than he already was. Brian only had so much energy."

It is my argument that Brian's failure to involve himself in heterosexual relations was to a large degree a consequence of his homosexual attractions. Brian died too young to resolve the enigma of his bisexual orientation, and was inhibited in its overt practice by the strictures of the generation in which he lived.

In the wake of meeting Pallenberg, Brian found himself facing Linda Lawrence's paternity suit over the birth of his son Julian. Brian's manner of dealing with Pat Andrews' public allegations of breach of marriage and association for their son Mark Julian was with the same sense of unreality as he brought to the Linda Lawrence situation. He assumed that if he psychologically blocked the issues, then they would go away. In his own mind he had acted aberrantly, but he refused to accept responsibility for the reality of both paternity suits. Brian's sexual pattern pre-1965 seems to have been dictated by pronounced misogynist traits. In the years when he was sexually active, he would make a woman pregnant, and then disown the relationship. His inveterate fear of commitment conformed both to the profligacy of the decadent libertine, and to the random sexual opportunism of gays who are into numbers. What Brian needed from women was an endorsement of adoration for his public image, and a sisterly protectiveness on the level of emotional bonding. Brian venerated beauty in women, and correspondingly feared to de-idealise the aesthetic by entering into sexual relations. He regarded the latter as a defilement of essentially visual attraction. Pallenberg looked like Brian and that in itself was sufficient reason for him to co-habit with her.

In fact on the night that Pallenberg was to meet Brian – the occasion was the band's 1965 Munich concert – she encountered a lachrymosely distraught Jones, who was desperate to take refuge in her sympathy. Pallenberg relates how: "There had been some kind of disagreement within the Stones. Brian against the others, and he was crying. He said, 'Come and spend the night with me. I don't want to be alone.' So I went with him. Almost the whole night he spent crying. Whatever had happened with the other Stones, it had absolutely devastated him."

By the time the Rolling Stones toured America and Canada in October 1965, Brian's nervous health had begun to collapse. He had to be hospitalised for a number of days in Chicago, with the medical indictment that if his alcoholism continued he would be dead within a year. Brian's ferocious cocktail of whisky and amphetamines made his violent mood swings unmanageable. Infrastructural pressures within the band, together with Brian's growing antipathy to the risks involved in live performances which incited riots, were in part responsible for the irregularity of his stage appearances. Under the spotlights the panda circles surrounding his eyes provided a commentary on his nocturnal lifestyle. Brian had grown to resemble the dissolute Count Eric Stenbock, who converted night into day, and whose stoned features were as memorable a psychogeographic of self-abuse as Brian's were to his immediate contemporaries.

Brian had also made his first visit to Marrakesh in 1965, and was fascinated by the hashish-smoking culture he encountered. Morocco, and more particularly Tangier, was the home of ex-patriate writers like Paul and Jane Bowles, a liberated capital which had attracted to its culture the seminal Beat writers, William Burroughs and Brion Gysin. Brian's immediate penchant for luxurious cushions, kaftans and tapestries, as well as a variety of Berber jewellery, was assuaged by the teemingly colourful Moroccan souks. He was to return to London with chests full of possessions and, just as importantly, with an inspired passion for the indigenous music he had heard played by street musicians in Marrakesh. The melodies they achieved, sitting on the ground playing native pipes, or producing African rhythms on percussion, was to make a profound impression on Brian's musical unconscious. It was from Brion Gysin that Brian first derived his knowledge of the Master Musicians of Jajouka, who lived in the foothills of the Rif mountains. Brian became intoxicated with his mentor's obsession with a music which pre-dated Islam, and began to conceive of ideas of integrating their sound into the Stones's music. It was to be another two years before Brian was to make the pilgrimage to the Rif mountains to record the Jajouka, but his creative sensibility was excited by the insidiously seductive music which pervaded every alley in Marrakesh.

Brian's inspired Moroccan interlude was, however, to be shadowed by a violent domestic scene. In their room at the Hotel Minzah, a mutually vicious and hysterically recriminative run-in between Brian and Anita resulted in Brian breaking his hand in rage against the metal window frame. He was to return to England temporarily incapacitated and unable to play guitar. Brian's smokily stormy relationship with Pallenberg was renowned for its furnacing aggression on both sides. Brian's friend, the antiquarian, Christopher Gibbs, who accompanied the couple to Morocco has recalled how: "They fought about everything – cars, prices, restaurant meals. Brian could never win an argument with Anita, although he always made the mistake of trying. There would be a terrific scene with both of them screaming at each other. The difference was that Brian didn't know what he was doing. Anita did."

A relationship in which each partner both provokes and is attracted to the other's shadow is destined for catastrophe. The incident in Morocco was to cost Brian dearly. He was never again to regain his esteem in a band who had come to view him as a wilful liability to their continuity as a touring force. Brian returned to London as a casualty, and was thereafter to orchestrate a regime of self-destruction which was to result finally in his dismissal from the Rolling Stones, shortly before his brutal murder on 2 July 1969.

TWO: **BISEXUAL PEACOCK**

"The pride of the peacock is the glory of God."

—William Blake

None of Brian Jones's four biographers seem to have attached sufficient importance to his undoubtedly bisexual orientation. I believe that Brian's licentiousness with women, in the pre-impotence phase of his dramatically chaotic life, was more a manifestation of misogynist impulse, than a proof of libidinous heterosexuality. Again, I want to draw the analogy with Oscar Wilde. Wilde met his future wife, Constance Lloyd, in 1883, and married her the following year, at a time when his finances were precarious, and the idea of domestic solvency by way of marriage to a financially secure partner, appealed to his aesthetic. In characteristically florid prose, Wilde was to describe Constance as, "a grave, slight, violet-eyed little Artemis, with great coils of heavy born hair which make her flower-like head droop like a blossom, and wonderful ivory hands which draw music from the piano so sweet that the birds stop to listen to her". Wilde is of course engaged here in aspecting metaphors for a bisexual ideal. Constance, in Wilde's apprehension, conforms to a poetic key-boarding of the idealised androgyne. Wilde was to dutifully have two children from the enamoured Constance, while at the same time pursuing at first an actively duplicitous gay life, and later an overtly public one in which caution was sacrificed for the risk of coming out. Even during the occasion of Wilde's honeymoon in Paris, he was to leave Constance at the hotel, and go out with his friend Robert Sherard in pursuit of the dangers to be encountered with lowlife.

Sherard tells us: "I think that it was during his stay in Paris at this time that he visited with me the haunts of the lowest criminals and poorest outcasts of the city, the show-places of the Paris Inferno – Père Lunette's and the Château-Rouge – which everybody who wishes to know the depths of darkness which exist in the City of Light goes to see."

Through his wit, sensitivity and essential vulnerability as a bisexual man, Wilde seems to have succeeded in making Constance into a companion, rather than a lover. Theirs was an unusual marriage at a time when women were ruthlessly subjugated to male authority. There's every reason to believe that Constance in part condoned Wilde's homosexual relations, and may well have been a confidante to his extra-curricular activities. Even after the scandal surrounding his imprisonment, and the social ruin which came to her as a consequence of her husband's disgrace, Constance continued to offer Oscar financial and moral support. Wilde's example is not uncommon. A man with homosexual propensities may attempt to regularise his unorthodoxy by seeking refuge in heterosexual relations. It's not so much a way out, as a stab at compromise. In Wilde's case marriage provided a social convention behind which he would hide with increasing resentment at the strictures modifying his gay identity. Wilde was finally to grow so contemptuous of having to repress his sexual instincts that he blew the game with self-destructive vengeance. He was openly seen in courtship with Lord Alfred Douglas, and defiantly took his pick-ups from the Piccadilly meat-rack to the hotels and restaurants that he would normally have reserved as meeting places for his aesthetically elitist circle. Wilde wanted to shock the world for the repressions he had been made to endure, and the effeminacy of his clothes, hair-do, and camply irreverent mannerisms were one way to implement the process. Wilde came out after the publication of *Dorian Gray* in 1891, and for the next four years proceeded to flaunt his difference to a seethingly hostile public. In the way that a militant post-war generation would have had Jagger and Jones incarcerated for daring to push gender definition beyond acceptable frontiers, so Wilde's generation saw it as their moral duty to have Oscar put away. Wilde the playwright was altogether too successful for his contemporaries to tolerate, and this coupled with his arrogant condemnation of the status quo created enemies in high places.

We learn a great deal about Brian Jones's bisexual makeup in the context of the book written by his friend, Nicholas Fitzgerald. *The Inside Story Of The Original Rolling Stone* is Nicholas's account of a friendship with Brian which spanned the last four years of the musician's life. Fitzgerald, a Guinness heir, was only seventeen when he first met the musician feted for his flamboyant looks, and he unequivocally tells us: "On July 24, 1965, I met and fell in love with Brian Jones. I was seventeen years old, living with my parents, and I had taken my girlfriend Marilyn to an elegant party in Royal Leamington Spa". Fitzgerald proceeds to tell us that the guests maintained an air of shocked silence in Brian's company, and that his sartorial palette comprised, "a pink and blue blazer, yellow pants, and blue shoes", and that the refinement of his accent was analogous to a public school drawl. Fitzgerald's response to first seeing Brian was one of sexual arousal, and in the naive prose in which the book is written, he succeeds in conveying the erotic charge which Brian apparently transmitted to both sexes. Fitzgerald writes: "Marilyn suddenly lost control and started squealing like a fan. Sensing my anger, Brian said, 'It's all right, I have that effect on women.' He gave me a hot look, clearly implying, 'and men, too'. I started to look away but didn't. His steady, caressing gaze was arousing me. It was the kind of rush that, until then, I had associated only with desire for a woman's body. He looked almost exactly like Marianne Faithfull, whose pictures I had seen in newspapers, and it occurred to me now that she and Brian could be twins. It was the face of a beautiful woman, yet Brian was macho enough. Marianne was utterly feminine, Brian the masculine version of her blonde, symmetrically featured type. I felt the unmistakable stirrings of an erection, quite a shock in those pre-liberation days, especially to a Roman Catholic boy."

What evolved from this felicitous intersection of two lives, was the beginnings of a friendship which seems to have involved occasional sexual relations. The infatuated Nicholas found himself, due to lack of bedroom space for guests, having to sleep on the floor that night parallel to Brian, each of them in respective sleeping bags. He quotes Brian as propositioning him with the motif, "It's a pity we don't have a double bed", before issuing him with a request to come and stay with him at his Fulham mews cottage. Nicholas was soon to find himself in the process of having to invent excuses to his girlfriend for his sudden and capricious disappearances whenever Brian suggested that they should meet. On their first date, Nicholas met Brian at the London Hilton, and from this location they went on to rendezvous at Flanagan's Bar, off Kensington High Street, and from there Brian drove his youthful prodigy in a Mini Moke to his mews behind the ABC Cinema on Fulham Road. Nicholas describes a mews tastefully furnished in Regency style, with long velvet curtains at the windows. A sophisticated interior, no matter the vestigial debris attendant on Brian's lack of attention to unused dishes and clothes spilled out of wardrobes onto the floor. Brian's general inability to cope with practical functions meant that he lived in a state of self-created chaos, and visitors to his succession of London residences were all to comment on the frenetic disorder of his living arrangements. Brian's permanent state of nervous exhaustion, exacerbated further by alcohol, was of course the reason for the accumulative mess in which he lived. Even the seventeen-year old Nicholas Fitzgerald was quickly aware of Brian's dysfunctional traits, although he is careful in his reminiscences never to demythicise his hero.

Brian quickly made it known to Nicholas that he shared the mews with Dave Thompson, and that the sleeping arrangements were flexibly ambidextrous. As a form of cajoling allurement, Brian was to suggest to Nicholas, "'You'll have to take up my offer to stay some time, then you'll find out for yourself'. Deliberately trying to catch my eye, he added, 'Won't you?'."

Brian was to leave Nicholas to his own devices, while he fetishistically washed his hair, and then proceeded to walk around the mews shirtless, his naked torso signalling impulses to Nicholas's groin. But the subtle balance informing Brian's bisexual machinations had him contrive to draw Nicholas's girlfriend, Marilyn, into the plot. Inviting the couple to have dinner with him at the Lotus House, 61 Edgware Road, Brian professed a sexual interest in both Nicholas and Marilyn, and from behind the facade of brandy intoxication, suggested that they should have a threesome. Brian's libertine proposal was rejected by the morally offended Marilyn, whose retort to Nicholas's sanctioning of the idea was: "'You go with Brian. You seem to like him more than you like me. Sounds as if you've been to bed together already anyway'."

Brian's constant need to confide in a trusting ear was to have him download his problems to Nicholas. As though obsessed with the idea of the unholy triumvirate of Jagger, Richards and Oldham scheming to undermine his authority within the band, Brian was to find in the seventeen-year old Nicholas, an at first puzzled, but later highly sympathetic ear. With his precarious hold on reality often deserting him, Brian's innate vulnerability could assume menacing proportions. Brian had learnt to trust nobody within his professional milieu. If he lived inwardly in a state of psychic fragmentation, then he translated his inner turmoil into an equally turbulent means of dealing with reality. The disorganised state in which Brian lived, observing no sense of time, arriving late or not at all for studio sessions and conducting his life according to eccentric principles, was almost an admission that his life would be of short duration. Rainer Maria Rilke's line in the *Duino Elegies*, "We live our lives for ever taking leave", is directly pertinent to those who die young, the ones whom Rilke chose to call "the early dead". And if Brian was fascinated by possessions, and seemingly compelled to purchase antiques and clothes with the obsessiveness of a collector, then he took little care of the items he so relentlessly purchased. His silks and velvets rainbowed across chairs and tables, the clothes discarded after having been tried on or worn for a single occasion. Food platters and glasses stained fragile, lacquered tabletops. Brian seems to have wanted everything and to have valued nothing, and the wealth at his disposal was the tool by which he could satisfy his impulse for instant purchases. Inwardly his only fulfilment was to express himself creatively, but the frustration attendant on finding those energies blocked or curtailed drove him increasingly to take refuge in acquiring material possessions.

Nicholas Fitzgerald asserted a beneficially calming influence on Brian. Nicholas movingly relates how on his last visit to Brian at Cotchford Farm, he attempted to take hold of Brian's hand and stroke it, as was his way in comforting his friend. But on this occasion Brian was too distraught to respond to a familiar gesture established by their relationship. Such moments of tenderness are invariably absent from the broken relationship reportage elicited from the women who played important roles in Brian's life. It is this author's opinion that Brian's emotional palette was brought into more sensitively colourful play in his relations with men, than in the phallocentric stance that he seems to have felt compelled to adopt in relations with women. Brian's behaviour with women manifested distinct traits of misogyny, chauvinism, dissociation from commitment, and a cold sense of detachment from emotional involvement. His adoption of feminine characteristics was in large motivated by a narcissistic impulse to become the woman who answered to his fantasy ideal. By successfully emulating women, Brian was on a psychological level clearly attempting to deny their existence in his life. The underlying contentious challenge to women implicit in male transvestism is one that Brian exploited to the full. The notion that men can do it better, and in the process of dressing up out-feminize their rival counterparts in little details of glam style, has always been one of drag's saliently outstanding features. While Brian formed relationships with women like Anita Pallenberg and Suki Potier, who were essentially his look-alikes, it was always he who dressed the more spectacularly, and won visual acclaim for clothes and a hairdo which out-rivalled his girlfriends in terms of ostentation.

Brian obviously felt happiest when cultivating his transvestite impulses. No matter Jagger's adoption of the sixties' unisex repertoire of colourful Carnaby Street clothes, he was never prepared to go as far as Brian in terms of female impersonation. There's always the feeling that Jagger was intent on shocking authority through his androgynous appearance, whereas with Brian you know that his choice of clothes was compatible with his femininity. Brian lived like a ruined blues queen who would auto-combust, rather than burn out slowly. His bathroom was stocked with pharmacy analgesics, while his fridge was full of liquid methedrine. What seems astonishing in retrospect was that there seemed to be nobody with sufficient sensitivity around Brian to help extricate him from his devastatingly unhealthy lifestyle. He seems to have been a classic victim of the sort of parasitism which stood to gain from actively encouraging his excesses. All the information collected about Brian Jones over the past three decades points to the loneliness and insecurity he experienced in his traumatic years of stardom. He was terrified of being abandoned in his state of nervous distress, and would on occasions pay for the company of a call girl to visit his apartment, solely to have a human presence, rather than face the solitary watches of the night alone.

Brian's friend Janie Perrin has related occasions on which Brian telephoned her in the night threatening suicide. Troubled by the deepening isolation he felt within the Stones's organisation, and paranoidly obsessed with the idea of being imprisoned for drug offences, Brian was both hysterical and desperate in his demands for help. "He was extremely unhappy," Perrin relates. "One of the times he was in the Dorchester Hotel, and he said he was going to throw himself out of the window. I said something like, 'Well, dear, go down a few floors before you do it. You don't want to make too much mess on the pavement.' 'Oh you're so terrible,' Brian told me... it was the same the second time when he was determined to slash his wrists and I told him to go into the bathroom first so as not to splatter blood on the bedroom carpet. I was 99 percent sure that he didn't really mean it, and I always tried to be firm, but light with him."

The hysteria inherent in Brian's behaviour was symptomatic of someone who felt unloved, and emotionally devoid of the reassuringly supportive qualities which are usually a part of relationships. One could argue that Brian's inner identification with desertion placed him in the role of an abandoned woman. Neither Anita Pallenberg nor Suki Potier seem to have been even partially successful in providing Brian with a secure emotional base from which to come to terms with his inner problems. At moments of deep crisis Brian seems always to have found himself in the desperate position of having to rely on the support of friends or acquaintances, or anyone who happened to be there at the time. Brian's complex psychology was such, that he both longed for the emotional bonding denied him by judgmental patents, while nonetheless resisting intimacy in relationships. There is evidence of deep guilt on his part in relations with women, as though he felt he was betraying his repressed homosexuality by entering into straight sexual discourse. Brian would be violent to women if they came too close, and under provocation he punched Anita Pallenberg in the face in a London night-club, as a means of targeting his resentment on someone he identified as a vampirical clone.

Some of the more problematic aspects of Brian's psychological behaviour seem to have issued from the conviction that life as a successful pop star exempted him from ordinary behaviour. Brian had always considered himself to be endowed with a creative mission, and when his ambitions were realised on a global scale for which he had never reckoned, he felt justified in acting out megalomaniacal tendencies. In a very real sense, success is invariably the enemy of creativity, and one could argue that as a musician Brian would have been better served playing on the small jazz and blues club circuit which provided his beginnings as a professional musician. Blues as a music had no precedent for the sort of crowd hysteria generated by the Rolling Stones. Brian was in many ways a victim of his own success. By introducing an effeminate visual appeal to their stage presence, and through injecting heady sexually overtones into their performance, the Rolling Stones had succeeded in revolutionising blues as a historic modality. Up until 1964, and before the Stones channelled their dynamic into mainstream pop, Brian was able to cope with the pressures attendant on fame. From 1965 onwards, he considered himself to be little more than a player of hybrid R&B pop, a form of musical expression which he considered to be a compromise in the interests of commercialism. But while Brian enjoyed the hedonistic lifestyle which accompanied the measures of fame, he remained at heart an R&B purist, and something of his perverse contempt for the band's success in music was expressed by his gradual withdrawal from their mainstream sound. Brian was at heart a bohemian, someone who had been prepared to suffer poverty and material hardship for his music, and his angular maverick spirit was ill-adjusted to the compromises necessary to be a pop star. He considered the Rolling Stones to have turned their backs on a legitimate creative dynamic.

Something of Brian's misogyny and the uncaring sides of his nature are related by Marianne Faithfull in her memories of life at Courtfield Road. Faithfull recounts an incident of Linda Lawrence arriving at Brian's address, and appealing from the street for child support for the two-year old Julian, who Brian had fathered. With imperious disrespect for the couple, Brian denied them entrance and held court from his balcony. Faithfull relates how "Brian and Anita just peered down on them as if they were some inferior species. Foppish aristocrats in their finery jeering at the *sans culottes* below. Upstairs everyone was laughing about it. It was so appalling, like something out of a Mexican folk tale, but Anita and Brian seemed to enjoy every minute of it."

This particular incident tells us a lot about Brian's disconnection from reality. The impression we gain of him through Faithfull's recollections is not of an uncaring or sadistic individual, but more as someone who had exempted himself from involvement in basic human issues. Rather like the Emperor Heliogabalus, Brian was more concerned with the highlights in his hair than he was with the deprivations of an illegitimate child. In his recreation of Heliogabalus' life, the French iconoclast Antonin Artaud writes of the monomaniacal Emperor: "I see a dangerous megalomania, both for others and the one who surrenders to it, in the fact of changing one's robe every day and of placing on each robe a jewel, never the same, which corresponds to the sign of heaven. There is in this much more than a taste for expensive luxury or a propensity for unnecessary waste – there is evidence of an immense, insatiable fever of the mind, which has a taste for metamorphoses. Whatever the price that must be paid for them, or the risk thereby incurred."

And wasn't Brian someone who pursued an endless chain of metamorphoses in his quest to reinvent himself through the adoption of a female persona? Despite Brian's conservative upbringing, he had managed by the age of twenty to free himself of all pre-conditioned traits of masculinity. He had effectively recreated himself, much to his parents' consternation, and was prepared to face the hostility directed at him by a general public unwilling to sanction effeminacy in men.

Brian was to prove instrumental to breaking up Nicholas Fitzgerald's relationship with his girlfriend Marilyn. "Why can't a woman be more like a man, as the song says," Brian was to put to Nicholas in questioning Marilyn's possessive behaviour. Confused by the irrepressible sexual attraction he felt for Brian, the teenage Nicholas attempted to clarify his feelings for his friend by questioning: "Was I gay? Bisexual? Society said either one was bad, what was I going to do about myself? Brian was always coming on to me, and yet there were always his girls. Perhaps if I had been older, more experienced and capable of taking the lead, Brian and I would have been in a deep love affair by now. Brian was flirting indiscriminately with everyone, and everyone was losing – often the dilemma of bisexuals."

Insights into Brian's lugubrious sexual relations with men are rare, largely because the women whom Brian rejected have coloured the text of successive biographies. Faithfull suggests in her auto-biography that at the time of her first meeting with Brian, she surmised that Jagger's complicity with the Stones's manager, Andrew Loog Oldham, was based on the premises of a gay relationship. If either Mick Jagger of Brian Jones had come out of the closet in the formative years of the sixties, the effects on the band's future would have been catastrophic.

Fitzgerald goes on to relate how the contentious jealousy that existed between Jagger and Jones extended to the domain of sexual partners. Nicholas, in his vivid portrayal of the antagonistic rivalry established between the two men, recounts an incident in which their hostility spilled over into contained rage on Jagger's part. Nicholas tells us: "Then Mick saw Brian, with his arm around this handsome young man, and me sitting opposite him, and he stopped dead in his tracks. His face turned pale, his overstuffed lips parted, and anger and jealousy were written all over him... Here he was with an attractive, long-haired girl with a peach of a figure – and he was jealous of Brian sitting with two young men. It seemed to me that he was so indecisive he couldn't even decide whether his proclivity was for girls or boys. Even if it was for both – as in Brian's case as well as my own – then surely he could stick to one at a time."

What is telling here, even given Nicholas's ill-concealed dislike of Jagger, is the confirmation he offers of Brian's homosexual propensities. He speaks as one who has experienced gay relations with Brian, and imparts to his statement the natural authority of a lover's shared experience.

Homosexuality in Britain was not decriminalised until July, 1967, when at the instigation of the Wolfenden Report, a Bill was passed which endorsed homosexual acts undertaken in private by two consenting men of twenty-one years of age or over. But the acting Labour Home Secretary Roy Jenkins was careful to caution any foreseeable celebrations over the outcome of the vote by advising the public that the sanction was in no way "a vote of confidence or congratulation to homosexuality". Other than afford individuals statutory rights to conduct gay relations in private, nothing had outwardly changed in a political context. Discrimination and homophobia were still entrenched in the prevailing social climate. Most gay men in the interests of professional demeanour were forced to comply with heterosexual ideals. Within the infrastructure of radical socio-sexual changes, the Rolling Stones were to play an important part in subverting gender roles in the gradual move towards sixties liberation. Brian was understandably supportive of measures of homosexual reform, and had he lived may even have come out in the more tolerant 1970s.

Across the Atlantic it was the death of Judy Garland in June 1969, which precipitated the Stonewall riots. Garland had represented an iconic materfamilias to generations of gay cabaret and drag artistes, her torchy stage act and hedonistic lifestyle having been construed as a metaphor for the persecuted gay individual. In Britain and America Judy Garland had come to be seen as the Patron Saint of Liberation. Following a police raid on the Stonewall Inn, a bar well known for its homosexual clientele, hundreds of rioting gay protesters rampaged through Greenwich Village giving voice to a newly acquired expression of power. The lid was dramatically blown off a century of overt persecution of gay rights, and gesture politics on a smaller scale were to be manifested in Britain the following year, when the first gay rights march took place in the capital.

I mention these apocalyptic events in the gay calendar, as they occurred during Brian Jones's lifetime, and because Brian was indirectly reflected in the turbulent mirror of social changes. But in the same way as the pointedly effeminate Quentin Crisp was made unwelcome in the gay ethos of London in the 1940s and '50s, due to his drawing unwanted attention to faggotry, so Brian's androgynous persona was too camply outré to find a resonance in London's homosexual underworld. Brian's appearance, while it was acceptable on stage, was thought too shocking to be assimilated with street politics. Brian, dressed in a frilly shirt, a purple velvet jacket and gold trousers, was even by sixties standards considered suspect. Operating within a select milieu, and conveyed from one destination to another in a chauffeur-driven Rolls Royce, Brian was spared confrontation with potential gay-bashers. His accepted means of protecting his trans-gender characteristics was invariably to be seen in the company of glamorous women. For a vulnerably feminine man, the best method of neutralising hostility towards his appearance, is to have the sanctioning company of a woman in attendance. One could hardly imagine Brian walking round London's less salubrious districts after closing time, and being unmolested by the vicious camaraderie aroused in a gang by intolerance of gays.

The question of male vulnerability and its isolation in the crowd is one brought into prominence by the distinction between performer and spectator. Sixties pop stars, and none more so than the Rolling Stones, adopted a manner of dress that often came close to drag. It has been pointed out that while the Rolling Stones predominantly dressed in clothes purchased from boutiques in Carnaby Street or the Kings Road, they combined those items with accessories like jewellery, scarves, makeup and fur coats, which went a long way to feminise unusual, but standard purchases. Brian would buy period clothes at the Chelsea Antique Market, but most of his accessories were obtained from female department stores. The stage has always been about the presentation of illusion, and up to a point the dissolution of gender roles, and within the precinct of the performance space Brian's appearance could at least be partially condoned by a hostile public. Performance is after all about the exaggeration of human ideals, and so the entertainer's costume is paramount to the visual success of the show. But what is considered pardonable by male orthodoxy in relation to an entertainer's prerogative to dress for the stage, is considered massively unacceptable on the street. Four decades of the general public being exposed to the fantastic costumes worn by pop stars on stage has done little to modify male hostility towards those who would wear such clothes out of context. It was all right for Mick Jagger to wear Mary Quant's scarlet eye shadow, or for Brian to sport hints of apricot and blue, but for street wear the arena radically changes into a space fraught with homophobic threat and male-pack aggression. Quentin Crisp has in his autobiography *The Naked Civil Servant* provided a courageous but devastating picture of the ignominy and insult he suffered from the London crowds in a lifetime of wearing makeup and feminine clothes in public. Brian Jones's costumes were spectacularly more attention-seeking than Crisp's, and while the latter derived from rejection a hard-won philosophy of being an individual at all times, no matter the force of opposition, Brian's sheltered life as a pop star saved him from encountering the immediate enmity of which Quentin Crisp was so often the victim. When Brian appeared with the Rolling Stones in their 1967 Palladium concert, his choice of clothes – a white broad-brimmed woman's hat, an elaborate cravat pinned with a large jewelled brooch, and a long jacket with a velvet collar additionally decorated by costume jewellery – he was unconsciously emulating Quentin Crisp's inveterate style of dressing. Quentin's blue period, that is his presentation of himself upwards of the age of forty, has over the years served as an interface between drag and the wardrobe adopted by sixties pop stars.

When Nicholas Fitzgerald visited Brian at the time of the Monterey Festival in 1969, he was to be witness to Brian's inordinate love of jewellery. Intimate with Brian in the latter's hotel bedroom, Fitzgerald writes of the exotically attired Brian: "Still smiling he got up and went to a drawer in an open trunk. He took out an elaborate gold necklace and draped it round his neck. 'Would I look less noticeable if I put on some jewellery? This is from Fifth Avenue in New York, from Saks. There's some more here. Come and see.' I stood beside him looking in the drawer. He was already wearing rings and bangles and brooches, but there was a whole treasure trove of the stuff in there. 'Got to keep up my image, you see. They're all dressing wildly gay now, especially here in San Francisco. Come on, let's go out and I'll show you.'"

Fitzgerald recounts how he and Brian went out into the streets, surrounded by bodyguards. Again, the clue here to Brian's being able to indulge to the full in his love of exotically decadent clothes, is the element of protection. Brian's privileged wealth as a pop star allowed him to circumvent the more brutal tenets of reality. In his years of success with the Rolling Stones Brian grew to be as divorced from reality as the debauched and despotic emperor Heliogabalus. It was said of Heliogabalus that he painted his face to resemble Venus, and that he dressed as a woman and covered himself with jewels, pearls, feathers, corals, and talismans. He would put on the solar tiara, dust his thighs with saffron and dip his penis in gold. He delighted in disguising himself as a prostitute, and in the costume of a rent boy would sell his body outside temples or in one of the squares. Heliogabalus's taste for ritual and theatre dissolved the boundaries between imagination and reality. His position of imperial power allowed him to live out his fantasies of posturing as a woman. The metaphor of the recurring decadent archetype was to find later embodiment in Brian Jones, who lived flagrantly, irresponsibly, and with the over-riding desire to intoxicate his senses. I'm not suggesting for a moment that Brian would have entertained the notions of political savagery that Heliogabalus saw fit to exercise, but more that the archetype which informed the despotic Emperor was in some way incorporated into Brian's particular sensibility. There's something about Brian, surrounded by security, and dressed as a woman, going out into the Californian streets at the time of the Monterey Festival in 1969, which finds an echo in the similarly dressed Heliogabalus being hunted to his death by Roman soldiers in the palace grounds. Both men risked revilement and murder as a consequence of stepping out of perceived gender roles, and both chose to be blondes in their exaggerated adoption of feminine identities. Brian's naturally aesthetic disposition delighted in the premises of sybaritic luxury. Whether he was idly nursing a sitar on a red counterpaned hotel bed, or dressed in a gold kimono while he fetishistically highlighted his hair, Brian favoured an interior world guarded by heavy velvet curtains, and an approach to reality cushioned by mind-altering substances. Marianne Faithfull portrays Brian as a foppish, correctly mannered eccentric, a Firbankian or Wildean individual, who if it wasn't for an incurable penchant for self-destruction via drugs and alcohol would have lived as a harmlessly affected decadent. If Brian hadn't been so diversely gifted as musician and so singularly driven by ambition, he might under different circumstances have evolved as a Crisp-like figure, all lavender eye shadow, floppy hats and tinted powder, walking the streets of Chelsea to the vicious commentary of ebulliently amused schoolchildren.

Brian's days were feminine ones in that they were without the need to conform to the ideological conception of male identity. The dictates of a capitalist society are such that men employed in most sectors of society are forced to obey principles of masculinity dictated by the status quo. Men employed in the arts have always supplied a variant to the rule, but in Brian's generation it was considered correct for the professions to have short hair, and to dress without traces of effeminacy. This ex-military code of uniformly presented masculinity is one that persists to this day in the standard professions, and the inability of men to quantify and evaluate the feminine components of their individual psyche is arguably one of the great tragedies of history. Warfare, fixed preconceptions of gender roles, blocked creative channels, the arrogant authoritarian assumption that men are superior to women, and all manner of aberrant psychological reasoning can be attributed to the rigid adherence to the notion of the conformist male. Brian was instrumental in helping to free a younger generation of the inherited misconceptions surrounding what it means to be a man. He was a catalyst to liberation, and as such should be remembered for the courage with which he delighted in subverting gender issues. Reacting against the fixed concept of male identity propagated by an immediate post-war generation, he succeeded in restoring colourful flamboyance to male appearance.

In his excellent study *Drag, A History Of Female Impersonation In The Performing Arts*, Roger Baker has this to say of the sixties generation in which Brian's presence was seminal to ringing the changes: "Because men were growing their hair longer," Baker writes, "and women were emulating the skinny bodies and Vidal Sassoon cropped hair of the models promoted by the new wave of photographers, something dubbed 'unisex' arrived to shock and entice. As far as drag went, however, this was a red herring: men never actually dressed as women nor women as men, but the concept did open up tentative discussion about the fascism of frocks and the tyranny of trousers."

The difference between Brian and say Danny La Rue, who was in the sixties making a national name for himself in the time-honoured tradition of drag, was that the latter excelled in female impersonation. La Rue, born Daniel Patrick Carroll in Cork in 1927, was by the sixties an almost permanent fixture in the West End. He represented the epitome of glamour in a nation accustomed to austerity, and while he owed his roots to British music hall and variety, La Rue grew to be an institution at a time when Brian Jones was exacerbating public tolerance by the wearing of white shoes and pink jeans. La Rue's ostentatious presentation of himself in frocks was again provided shelter by the sacrosanct precinct of the stage. Had he ventured out into Wardour Street still wearing drag he would doubtless have been the target of homophobic West End violence.

When the Rolling Stones played the Royal Albert Hall on September 23, 1966, Nicholas Fitzgerald was in attendance to keep a trained eye on Brian's choice of clothes for the occasion. According to Fitzgerald, "Brian was holding his own now with Mick as the star of the Rolling Stones. Brian was outstanding not only in his performance, but in his extravagant clothing. He wore a purple velvet jacket and a red shirt with a white cravat and grey trousers." When Nicholas was to first visit Brian at the musician's Courtfield Road apartment, he found Brian dressed in black cord trousers and a white frilly shirt, and in the process of selecting the gold bracelets to accent his tasteful costume. Fitzgerald quotes Brian as saying, "'I might look a bit of a poof, but the world needs to be brightened up a little, don't you think?'"

If Brian lived in the unreality of a mind-set cushioned from the external world by the physical presence of bodyguards, then the likes of Quentin Crisp were forced to live out their gender modifications on the street. Crisp was followed, hassled and insulted. Fortified by inexhaustible reserves of inner conviction, and a dignity maintained in the face of verbal abuse, Crisp learned to avoid eye contact with people, and to never answer back under provocation. Crisp embodied the pariah's role of being socially outlawed as a consequence of daring to violate protocol. That a little henna, foundation, eye shadow, mascara and lipstick applied to a man should invite such ridicule, and such harrowing threat to the wearer, is an issue that goes deep into the collective psyche. In the pre-pop years Quentin Crisp unwittingly represented the socially disinherited and the sexually outlawed. But his statement of appearance went much deeper than being merely a superficial assertion of gay rights. Crisp called into question the whole complex psychology of gender, quite independent of sexual orientation. Apart from a youthful period of working as a rent boy in London, Crisp has largely professed to being asexual, and while his mental sympathies are supportive of homosexuality, his passion for cross-dressing has more in common with a transvestism which finds sexual fulfilment in the act itself. Consummation for Quentin is in the makeup palette, and in the considerable risk exercised by daring to be a man dressed with feminine appeal.

Crisp's notoriety in London, before he took up residence in New York, where he has acted as a self-deprecating homosexual who hates other homosexuals, was written into the British sensibility sufficiently deeply for him to earn the privileged sobriquet of being called a "stately homo". Crisp was certainly a London sight at the time when Brian Jones was living in the Chelsea and Kensington boroughs. We have no record of Brian's knowing of the older man's existence, but if they had met they would have shared a striking resemblance in terms of their exhibitionistically parading the streets in Ascot hats, silk scarves, and scintillating pieces of costume jewellery.

Being camp usually implies not only a sense of the individual's social displacement, but also a condition of the protagonist's perceived spiritual isolation. Any study of Brian Jones will point to the essential isolation he felt as an individual. One suspects that he lacked the ability to be close with anyone. He complained of continual outsidership within the context of the Rolling Stones, and of feeling an auxiliary member of his own band. Brian lacked the ability to consolidate concrete relations – women invariably left him for reasons of his inherent narcissism – and, in the last weeks of his life he was to complain of oppressive loneliness, and of being held a prisoner in his own house. Brian had a natural propensity for arrogance, and it was often his air of conceit which won him enemies within the lower echelons of the Rolling Stones organisation. He knew his worth, both as a musician and as a revolutionary fashion leader, and it was his inability to conceal his sense of superiority that had him disliked by the tradesmen, chauffeurs and minders with whom he came into contact. Where Brian felt no sympathetic rapport with a person, then his natural code of defensiveness was to express himself through arrogance.

Being camp is also, as a state of self-magnification, a need in the individual to colour the canvas to an almost intolerable degree. Brian was one of those who felt compelled to mirror his rich inner life with a corresponding external image. The androgyne is invariably he who in the willingness to combine masculine and feminine, anima and animus within himself, unifies the distinctions in a composite appearance. But in doing so he may attract the savage hostility of the unsympathetic. Brian was kept under official surveillance because he drew attention to his unwillingness to conform. He was additionally unpopular because he carried non-conformity to excess and so drew attention to others who were clandestinely experimenting with illicit substances.

It was Neil Bartlett, who in his imaginatively inventive reconstruction of Oscar Wilde, *Who Was That Man?*, drew attention to the association between homosexuality and collecting. Brian Jones shared Oscar Wilde's compulsion to surround himself with pretty things. In Wilde's case the predilection was for art, as well as antiques, and Oscar's house in Tite Street, Chelsea, was full of possessions. Wilde owned drawings by the artists, Burne-Jones, Whistler, Monticelli and Simeon Solomon, and valued china, jewellery, and his library of rare editions in which bindings and limitation numbers were a necessarily precious vocabulary of the elitist aesthete. He took feminine pride in having the rooms decorated according to specific requirements. The library walls were to the height of 5'6", painted in dark blue distemper, with the ceiling provided for in gold. The second floor front bedroom was painted pink with the top of walls under the cornice apple green. Wilde's scheme for the drawing-room was a combination of ivory woodwork, the walls being distempered flesh pink, while the cornice was decorated lemon and gold.

Brian was similarly obsessed with making purchases of antiques for his London apartment, and later for the interior furnishings of Cotchford Farm. Friends who journeyed with him to Morocco spoke of the trunk-loads of brocade cushions, fabrics and items of Berber jewellery which Brian had transported home to Courtfield Road. Brian's inability to keep order in his London flat was largely the result of the inordinate number of party-goers who dropped in, and who in various degrees of alcoholic or drug disorientation failed to respect the elegantly furnished interior. That the effects of revelry resulted in ensuing domestic chaos were inevitable, and Brian's habitual state of chronic nervous exhaustion made it impossible for him to repair the nightly damage. At Cotchford Farm, under the attentive eye of his domestic Mary Hallett, Brian contributed to a more controlled household regime. Given time and opportunity he would doubtless have attracted a wealth of future collections to his femininely acquisitive person.

If Brian's active bisexuality was simply an expression of a deeper, more repressed homosexual state, then like Quentin Crisp Brian seems to have been moving towards adopting an asexual ideal, in which narcissism was in itself a form of sexual consummation. Brian's later relations with women seem to have involved companionship or psychic bonding rather than sexual fulfilment. Brian had discovered that his exaggerated displays of femininity had in part dispensed with the need for a female sexual partner. What Brian shared in common with Quentin Crisp, was the move towards creating a third sex, neither male nor female, and gender-bound towards an inverted fascination with self-love. Although Crisp has openly declared himself a homosexual, he is not attracted to men's bodies. I suspect that Brian too would have grown progressively towards a stage of rejecting physical contact with both sexes. He would have settled like Crisp into making himself into an untouchably preenish artefact.

Brian's placing within the modality of bisexual consciousness gave him strong archetypal associations with the god Dionysus. Within the concept of androgynous consciousness, male and female are psychologically united in what alchemists call a state of *coniunctio*. James Hillman has pointed out in his consideration of Dionysian aspects of psyche, *The Myth Of Analysis*, that: "One of the names for Dionysus was 'The Undivided', and one of his main representations was as child. The child refers to a view of reality which is not divided." This insight is valuable when applied to Brian's sexual psychology, for we tend to think of Brian as a perversely puckish child, a tantrum-throwing adolescent who never properly entered the world of adulthood. Brian made few concessions to the impositions of reality as they are defined by the socially structured adult world. When at the end of his youthful life he purchased Cotchford Farm, the former home of A.A. Milne, what thrilled Brian was to live in The House At Pooh Corner, and to bask in the rural shelter the house provided. A photograph of Brian pictured by the life-size statue of Christopher Robin in the garden, says it all. The retreat to Cotchford was also the chance for Brian to exorcise the occult jinx apparently put on him by Anita Pallenberg, and to attempt to regain contact with musical roots from which he had felt temporarily disinherited. One could almost say that Brian journeyed home to childhood in order to die.

An attraction to both sexes is very often co-extensive with the creative sensibility, and presents a problem to the individual only when feelings of guilt originating from moral pre-conditioning are brought into conflict with natural desire. As we know it, largely through the source of Nicholas Fitzgerald, Brian appears not to have entertained feelings of guilt about his bisexuality. In the ancient world, Plutarch tells us, the cult of the bisexual was worshipped with abandon. "At Argos," he says, "the chief festival of Aphrodite was called hysteria, and connected with the same form of the cultus was the strange hermaphroditic festival which bore the special name of the Feast of Wantonness, at which women dressed as men, and men as women, the men even wearing veils."

Brian paid service to the bisexual dominant, or what James Hillman rightly calls "the God of one's bisexuality. With truly insightful sympathy, Hillman extends his essay to the consideration that: "Our afflictions and pathologies evoke the feminine side as carrier, sufferer, as nurse to that sufferer and to the child. The feminine side also holds out joyful abandonment to them and so a release through them. Dedication of the affliction returns them to a connection with the archetype which is reaching us through these symptoms and psychopathologies." Hillman rightly goes on to argue that any attempt at extracting the active male aspect of suffering from the feminine passive one would result in a divided totality. Brian remained whole, and gave joyful embodiment to the bisexual ideal, both in his relations and in his dress. According to Plato, "the sum of all things is both at once", and the living out of this concept perfectly satisfies the attraction to both sexes.

As a decade, the sixties with its conflation of literary and pop cultures – the novels of Huysmans, Genet and Burroughs were read alongside the allegorically Utopian works of Hermann Hesse – incorporated decadence into its psyche, not only through literature, but through the adoption of Eastern drugs. Marianne Faithfull writes of the scene at Brian's Courtfield Road apartment, as though the company could have stepped out of a Huysmans novel. Faithfull describes it as: "A veritable witches' coven of decadent illuminati, rock princelings and hip aristos... Peeling paint, clothes, newspapers and magazines strewn everywhere. A grotesque little stuffed goat standing on an amp, two huge tulle sunflowers, a Moroccan tambourine, lamps draped with scarves, a pictographic painting of demons (Brian's)... There's Brian in his finest Plantagenet satins, fixing us with vacant, fishy eyes." Brian's immediate ethos cocktailed youthful hedonism with the belief in a future ideological Utopia. A new youth were determined to close the door on warfare, national poverty, conformity of dress, sexual discrimination, outmoded conventions, and the straitjacketing intolerance that stems from a rigidly applied monotheism. For a brief moment in mid-sixties Britain, anything and everything seemed possible. The liberal smoking of hashish and marijuana increased the tendency towards a pacifist vision in which warfare as the instrument of male aggression would be considered a thing of the past. Under the new regime, men with Brian's appearance simply didn't qualify to participate in military service.

Brian's close friend, Ronni Money, has spoken of the musician's vulnerability, and of the confusion he suffered over whether people valued him for himself or his identity as a pop star. Elaborating on Brian's emotionally debilitating relationship with Anita Pallenberg, Money has stressed: "Anita was into the bisexual number and arranged scenes ...Brian could be easily put upon if a person exerted certain emotional pressures. Female fans couldn't exert any pressure, because they were overawed by him. But when you could take or leave Brian the star (which was basically what he wasn't into), the minute you could sort of shrug your shoulder about it, he saw a ray of hope – as if to say, 'At least this person is accepting me for me. A fan wouldn't just take me or leave me.'"

Brian's manifold emotional confusions were all part of his anxiety temperament. A naturally refined introvert, Brian was obsessed with music to the exclusion of almost any other interest in life. How he connected with reality outside of his preoccupying creative dynamic was always on a secondary level. If Brian worked on the transformation of himself from male to female, then his androgynous creation of a unified self was something he saw as an extension of his music. Creativity is so polarised to bisexual consciousness, that one could justifiably claim that the two states are inseparable.

Returning to Oscar Wilde, and his life representing the lie which tells the truth; Wilde was hunted by the authorities because his lie was too calculatedly transparent. The decorously circumspect Mr. Wilde of Tite Street, Chelsea, the respected author of racily humorous

West End successes, was also the novelist of dark homosexual life depicted in *The Picture Of Dorian Gray*, and a notorious queen who consorted with rent boys in London's nocturnal underworld. Wilde, who confessed in 1897, "my life is a scandal," lived to attract and be broken by the authorities he so feared. Oscar fell, as though he had tumbled down the stairs at Kettners, into a police trap. A great deal of contrivance and scheming went into effecting Oscar's ruin. In the same way as Wilde had been forced to live duplicitously, so his investigators trapped him by judicial duplicity. There were no justifiable reasons for his conviction, and it took three separate trials to fabricate premises for his criminality. But minds all over London were scheming for a long time to bring about his ruin. He was being watched at the instigation of the Marquess of Queensberry. It was part of Oscar's individual destiny that he should suffer, in the same way as Brian Jones was to be tracked by the law, and forced into corners. But with both men the responsibility for their respective patterns of persecution would have originated at some point from a single individual. We know about Wilde's detractors, but who was the first person to encourage the idea of breaking Brian? There is undoubtedly somebody still alive who, having insighted Brian's fragility, and having calculated the profits of exploiting it, set in motion, perhaps casually at first, the idea that Brian should be destroyed. Evidence collected by Geoffrey Giuliano in *Paint It Black* and Terry Rawlings in *Who Killed Christopher Robin?* points conclusively to the fact that Brian was murdered. But the murder by drowning was the culmination of a chain of informer set-ups by which Brian was increasingly brought to the edge of mental collapse. In the same manner that Oscar Wilde was feared by his familiars in a clandestine gay coterie, for drawing attention to their existence by his temerity of dress, so too Brian's exaggerated clothes and reckless consumption of stimulants were considered bad news to those of his contemporaries with something to hide. The Rolling Stones had attracted the semi criminal underworld to its ranks of employees, as well as the usual contingent of parasitic dealers, and Brian found himself both threatened and exploited by this nefarious organisation. Education and class made it difficult for him to assert himself in base company. It was a vicious circle. The more paranoidly vulnerable Brian became, the more he took refuge in drugs and alcohol, and so set himself up to be manipulated by the unscrupulous. Geoffrey Giuliano, via the source of former Stones employee, Trevor Kempson, quotes the latter as naming the band's distinguished PR Les Perrin, as being responsible for Brian's gradual fall from grace. According to Kempson, he was "fairly sure those tips originated with Les Perrin. Also one or two of the Stones's drivers who had criminal records and were therefore vulnerable to police pressure and saw Jones as being a threat. They didn't like him much anyway and weren't unhappy at earning a little pin money. There was a good reason why Brian had to go, so far as (he was) concerned, and that was the problems he caused Jagger which resulted in him suing the *News Of The World*."

Brian became marked like the figure of the archetypal scapegoat. We could argue that he like Wilde was the more conspicuous for his bisexuality, and so better able to be sighted by the enemy. Unlike Wilde, Brian was denied any roominess of time or maturity in which to apply revisionist policies to his inner growth. He died at the first halt he had known in his intensely pressurised life as a member of the Rolling Stones, and with his future plans as a musician still only partially formed. Like Wilde, he paid a bitter price for his decadent lifestyle and uncompromising individuality, and like his predecessor in scandal he was to become the victim of authorised injustice.

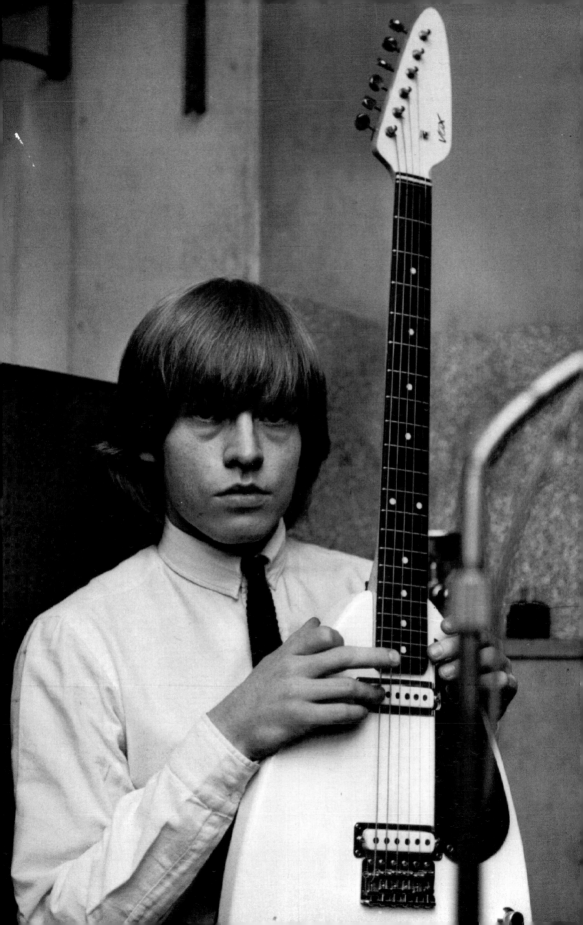

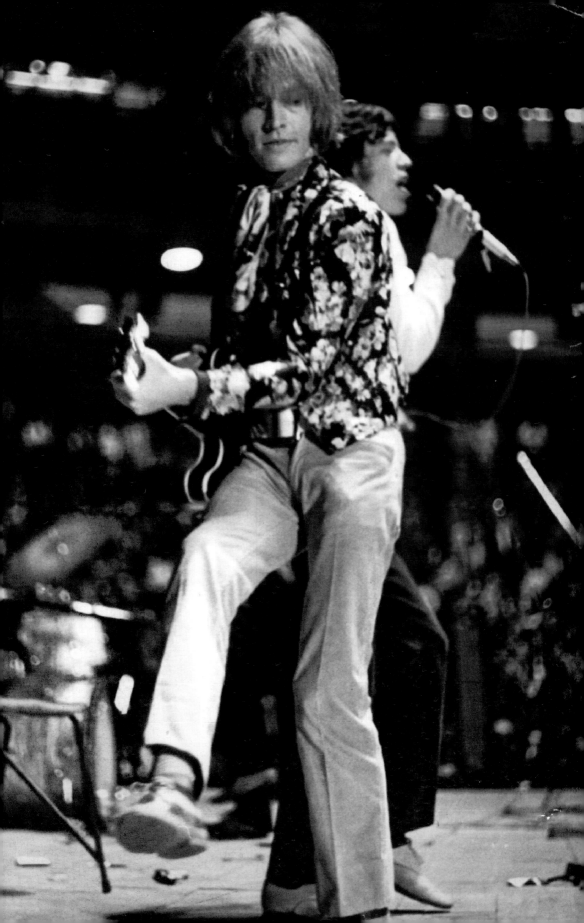

THREE: **SHE COMES IN COLOURS OF THE RAINBOW**

"It is not difficult to walk down Piccadilly carrying a lily; what is difficult is to make people think I did."

—Oscar Wilde

Betrayal, and all the attendant panic and breakdown to inner support structures that it brings, played a big part in Brian's life. Oscar Wilde once wrote that what we most fear almost inevitably becomes in time a reality. Wilde had lived in terror of being criminalised for his homosexuality, and whatever his inner presentiments of personal ruin, they were to be catastrophically realised by the events surrounding his trial in 1895. Wilde was to step into the authoritarian and depersonalising hell that he must have imagined would be a part of his individual destiny. One could argue that he was inexorably compelled by perverse inner dictates to confront the opposition. He was offered the opportunity to leave the country, but he refused.

Brian's sense of lifelong betrayal began in his teenage years. While still undergoing the buffeting traumas and emotional confusions common to teenage crisis, he was to return home one day to find his parents, who had meanwhile gone on holiday, had deposited all his belongings in a suitcase, and left it out in the garden. His early experience of being rejected by his parents, and finally dispossessed of a home was to contribute to the constant feelings of insecurity which undermined Brian as an adult. Brian's reaction to this incident was to turn his back on his parents, and to leave home for good. He was to take up residence at 73 Prestbury

Road in Cheltenham's student district, and to pursue his musical ambitions from the constrained space of a flat he shared with his friend, Dick Hattrell.

Brian's father was later to attempt to justify his formidable parental authority on the grounds that he never anticipated the success that would come to his son as a musician. It was the typical uncaring afterthought of a man who clearly resented his son's possession of an individual spirit, and yet who after Brian's death was to benefit from his estate. Not that Lewis Jones in his wilful desire to repress his son's creative expression, differed so greatly from a generation of men raised on the ideal of authoritarianism. Creativity has always been reviewed with suspicion by those who perceive it as a deviation from the capitalist ethic of work and family. Artists are primarily responsible to their creative vision, and may place secondary the material aspirations to secure income or regulate a family unit. Brian was understandably unwilling to commit himself to the system, and chose instead to take casual jobs, including being a coalman, as a means of financing his formative growth as a musician. His dislike of practical responsibilities was to extend to his early relationships with Pat Andrews and Linda Lawrence, both of whom were to conceive his illegitimate children, only to face rejection on the grounds that they were incompatible with his image as a musician. In her book *Golden Stone*, Laura Jackson describes an incident recounted by Pat Andrews, in which Brian, who had been two-timing Pat, was confronted by a hysterical Linda at the back of the building in Slough at which the Rolling Stones were playing. According to Pat Andrews: "Linda was actually on her knees in a puddle in front of Brian begging him not to finish with her, just because Mark and I had come on the scene. Brian was trying to haul her up, but she kept collapsing and clutching at him. He was upset too and telling her that it had to be off between them..."

Emotionally harrowing scenes were common in Brian's tempestuous private life. In this incident, unwilling to consciously hurt either woman, Brian succeeded in protracting their suffering by treating both partners as unreal. He seems only to have been able to enter into fantasy relationships, and once the reality of the situation presented itself with all its contingent responsibilities, his instinctual policy was to run away. Brian began families to which he had no intention of committing, and no interest in maintaining. These failed relations read like splinter attempts to conform to heterosexual orthodoxy, and were partnerships rejected by the narcissistic and homosexual components of Brian's oscillating sexuality. Marriage, with its conformist sense of settling down to parental duties, would have found alarming associations in Brian's mind with what he took to be the stagnation of his parents' lives in provincial Cheltenham. To have entered into family life would have been for Brian to have risked emulating a domestic template he despised. While he continued to retain contact with his family it was on the level of seeking their approval for his success as a musician. Brian was anxious to be accepted by his parents for his artistic identity. Part of the inherited parental/child conflict through the ages is the one in which the child feels manipulated by a parental desire to structure its ambitions according to their own. The rebellious generation of youth to whom Brian belonged were determined to reject superimposed values, and to renounce all allegiance to the social tenets taken on trust by their parents. Brian's quest for individual identity, although it may have proved more extreme than is the case with many of his contemporaries, was nonetheless part of the vision with which his age identified. The beginnings of rebellious youth in the 1950s, with the advent of stars like Marlon Brando, James Dean and Elvis Presley, had provided the archetype with which Brian identified. What had begun as a momentum of choppy surf in the fifties was to escalate to the proportions of a tidal wave as the sixties advanced. Societal values in large were overturned and questioned for the degree of truth or lies inherent in their concepts. A state-controlled Western monotheism was modified by the introduction of Eastern religious and meditational exercises into its canon. The collective changes as they occurred were also reflected in the individual. One doesn't have to be an archetypalist to see how big a part Brian Jones played in the social upheaval of the mid-1960s. Both as a visual icon of the newly prevailing androgynous image, and as a musician who transplanted black music into white culture, his place as an innovator is assured.

In terms of the psychological Brian, it is fruitful to keep in mind the independent psychiatric profile on him prepared by Walter Neustatter. Amongst his findings Neustatter was to note that Brian did not: "reveal signs of formal thought disorder or psychotic disturbances of thought processes. However, Mr. Jones's thought processes do reveal some weakening of his reality ties as a result of intense free-floating anxiety. He currently tends to feel very threatened by the world about him as a result of his increasingly inadequate control of aggressive instinctual impulses. This repressive control seems to be breaking down and he often resorts to conspicuous denial of the threat created by the breakthrough of these impulses into consciousness. At times he projects these aggressive feelings so that he feels a victim of his environment; at others he introjects them, resulting in significant depressive tendencies and associated suicidal risk."

The tendency to dissociate from reality, the repression of aggressive instinctual impulses, the propensity for depressive tendencies and to feel threatened by the environment were all psychological states with which Brian identified. Brian's refusal to accept adult responsibilities led of course to a succession of disastrous relationships. Central to these emotional catastrophes was the progressive difficulty he experienced in coping with reality. In many ways being a pop star was the only level on which Brian could function, for the role allowed him to live out his notion of being extraordinary.

The theme of betrayal in Brian's life was most closely linked to his attempts to form a more durable relationship with Anita Pallenberg. According to Geoffrey Giuliano, Pallenberg admitted to having put an occult spell on Brian by way of an effigial jinx. Moulding candle wax into a symbolic representation of her lover, she jabbed a needle into the lower stomach. Of her own admission: "The next morning I went back and found him suffering from severe stomach pains. He'd been up all night and was in agony, bottles of Milk of Magnesia and other medications all around him. The world of the occult fascinated me, as did witchcraft and the black magicians (Kenneth) Anger introduced me to."

Pallenberg's cultivation of the left-handed path, or the cult of the shadows, was to prove devastating to Brian's susceptibility to breakdown. Magic practised for the purposes of sensational power is, if the adept lacks correct initiation into the ascending hierarchies of knowledge, highly dangerous to karma. The acquisition of power in order to dispense evil – a practice arising from those who fail to properly assimilate Aleister Crowley's teachings – is always symptomatic of the fraud. Pallenberg's drug-cocktailed excursions into the peripheries of black lore were, with all their mismanagement of occult principles, lethal to Brian's precarious hold on sanity. A sixties generation viewed the practice of magic as an adjunct to drug culture. Brian's problem was that despite his attraction to altered states of consciousness as a respite from the reality he so feared, he was unable to cope with the effects of hallucinogenics on his brain chemistry. When on 18 December 1966, Brian suffered the death of his best friend, Tara Browne in a motor accident, his way of dealing with the situation was to take large quantities of Tuinols and Mandrax in the effort to alleviate his emotional suffering. The side effects of Brian's chosen chemicals were to be far more inhibitive to functioning than if he had faced his grief naturally. It has been suggested that Brian's relations with Tara Browne were of the same homoerotic nature as those he shared with his friend, Nicholas Fitzgerald.

Even if Brian, superficially interested in magic through Pallenberg's purchase on the subject, did have the registration plates for his Rolls Royce read: DD 666, or Devil's Disciple 666, it is unlikely that he acquired any serious occult mastery of power. 666, the number attributed to the Great Beast or the anti-Christ, was in his adopted vocabulary, simply an expression of decadence. Brian was a degenerate and not a Satanist. Brian's true soulmates were to be found in the likes of Charles Baudelaire, Count Eric Stenbock and Oscar Wilde rather than in the tradition of Aleister Crowley and his disciple Kenneth Anger. Anger, who seems obsessed with the concept of evil as a transmissible force, considered Brian to be a male witch endowed with the blemish of a supernumerary nipple. Anger has disclosed how Brian: "showed me his witch's tit. He had a super-numerary tit in a very sexy place on his inner thigh. Brian was the most psychic of the Stones. He saw the spirit world; for the others it was just the climate of the times. One gets the impression he just dissolved into it."

Anger's conjecture that Brian may have literally dematerialised into the ether is not as improbable as it sounds. From the position of inhabiting an etheric body on the astral plane, Brian has since his death succeeded in communicating to mediums. His bond with the spiritual world, begun during his lifetime, has continued as an extension of his post human identity.

Recalling Anita Pallenberg in Brian's Courtfield Road days, Marianne Faithfull has chronicled her memories as such: "Dazzling, beautiful, hypnotic and unsettling. Her smile – those carnivorous teeth! – obliterated everything. Other women evaporated next to her. She spoke in a baffling dada hipsterese. An outlandish Italo-Germanic-Cockney slang that mangled her syntax into surreal fragments. After a couple of sentences you became hopelessly lost.

God, did she just say that? She was either putting you on or this was the Delphic oracle. You were on your own, it was all part of her sinister appeal."

The word "sinister" seems pertinent to most contemporary profiles of Pallenberg's character. She was clearly a disaster-site for Brian's attenuated hold on his rapidly disintegrating sanity. Reports of Brian punching her in the face in a night-club, an act registering from extreme provocation, were instances when Brian unleashed the repressed aggression on which his psychiatrist had commented. It is sometimes a condition of love that we encounter a psychic adversary in the other. In Jungian terms Brian and Anita compounded the paradoxical criterion of representing each other's shadow. Each mirrored the other's potential for engagement with negative aspects of the psyche. Relationships like this often lead to a mutual form of soul murder, and Brian was not only left nervously drained by Pallenberg's intensity, but was also to undergo the experience of being vampirically spat out by her betrayal.

The story of Brian's betrayal has often been told, and it loses none of its terror in the retelling. In an archetypal sense, Pallenberg's role in the story was that of a vampirical Lilith. Lilith, who was a primordial succubus, also served as a protean form of metamorphic witch who had a deleterious effect on male psychic energy. Men are debilitated by contact with Lilith. Brian was effectively emasculated by his love-hate relationship with Anita Pallenberg.

According to the available facts, Keith Richards, Anita Pallenberg and Brian were chauffeur-driven by Tom Keylock to France, with the idea that they would convene with a group of friends at the Hotel Minzah in Tangier. They travelled in Richards' Bentley Continental on a tortuous, 2,000-mile route across France and Spain, gradually ascending into mountain ranges where Brian's asthma grew chronic. Unable to cope with the increasingly thin air and his psychological terror of mountains, Brian developed a high temperature and had to be hospitalised in Toulouse. With the prognosis one of suspected pneumonia, he was ordered to rest for a week. Without remorse, the group continued on their journey, leaving Brian to celebrate his 25th birthday alone in his hospital bed.

By the time the remaining party reached Valencia, Richards and Pallenberg had entered into a sexual liaison. Pallenberg returned to the hospital to accompany a justifiably paranoid Brian to their hotel base in Marrakesh. Brian's suspicions were immediately alerted when he observed the sympathetic exchanges and body language shared by Pallenberg and Richards. Brian knew intuitively that Anita intended to desert him, but he lived with the hope of proving his misconception a lie.

Up on the tenth floor of the Minzah, Brian began taking acid in the attempt to disengage from the bitter truth that he was in the process of losing Anita to his trusted friend Keith Richards. Searching for emotional support independent of the Stones party, Brian renewed contact with Brion Gysin, the writer/painter with whom he had formed a friendship on his previous Moroccan visit. According to Pallenberg, Brian beat her up in their hotel room, returned later in the day with two Berber whores, and was generally obnoxious to her in his drugged state of mind. With the threat of reporters about to arrive in Marrakesh in pursuit of the Rolling Stones party, it was considered wise to have Brian transferred to a rented house on the outskirts of the city. Appropriate to Brian, the big overgrown garden surrounding the house contained hundreds of peacocks. As a distraction from his uncomfortable domestic situation, Gysin decided to take Brian to the Djemaa El Fna – the town square – to record native music; and there Brian happily moved from musician to musician taping their indigenously narcotic sounds. Brian was quickly uplifted by the experience, and joined Gysin in smoking hashish with a number of local mystics.

Meanwhile, and unknown to the briefly euphoric Brian, the entire Stones party had checked out of the Hotel Minzah, leaving him disconsolately alone and on the edge of precipitant breakdown. Tom Keylock, who was euphemistically called a minder, and who had apparently stage-planned the betrayal, had driven Richards and Pallenberg out of Marrakesh to Tangier where they boarded a ferry for Malaga, thereafter taking a plane from Madrid to London. And without any consideration for Brian's abandonment, Keylock returned to London by Bentley with the cool indifference of a man insensitive to the appalling predicament in which he had placed Brian.

On his return to the hotel Brian was confronted with the news that his party had deserted him. In a state of hysterical panic Brian managed to telephone Brion Gysin, who immediately came to his friend's assistance, and instructed the hotel to call a doctor. Gysin was understandably frightened that Brian would either have a nervous seizure or become so out of control that he would injure himself. A doctor duly arrived and sedated the distraught musician.

Brian had been made the victim of a merciless act of betrayal, but the connivance behind the scenes was such that he had lost his girlfriend to a colleague with whom he would have to interact on a day to day basis. He was understandably shattered, and the increased sense of self-esteem he had experienced during the time of his relationship with Pallenberg, was quickly negated. Emerging from the effects of sedation, Brian telephoned his friend Ronni Money in London, and informed her that he had not only been deserted, but that his friends had stolen his cash, credit cards and valued cameras. Brian somehow survived the night by making frantic and largely incoherent calls to friends. With money sent to him by the Rolling Stones office, and in desperate need of consolation, Brian headed for his friend Donald Cammell's flat in Paris. Cammell opened the door on his emotionally overwrought friend to find him visibly broken and without luggage. In his shocked state, all Brian could do was to keep on incredulously repeating the mantra: "They left me."

Taking refuge with his friend for the night, and compulsively drinking copious amounts of spirits, Brian fortified himself in preparation to returning to London the next day. That he was in no condition to face the journey unaccompanied seems to have occurred to nobody, and Brian who was superficially an idol to hundreds of thousands of fans, characteristically found himself facing the crisis alone. All the meaningless surface glitter of fame must have been apparent to Brian as his raging insecurities took over. He had not only irreparably lost a valued relationship, but his future with the Rolling Stones had been put in considerable jeopardy by the almost untenable position in which Brian was now placed. Within the power infrastructure of the band Jagger and Richards now were indomitable, and Brian was to view his betrayal in Morocco as still another step towards his eventual dismissal from the band.

It was a panic-stricken and dissociated Brian who returned to London in search of Pallenberg. Unknown to Brian, whose desperation increased by the hour, Richards and Pallenberg had gone into hiding together in a St. John's Wood flat, and were not to emerge for a week. Brian's incessantly frantic telephone calls across London met with no success in his attempts to locate Pallenberg's whereabouts. When Brian at last made contact with Anita, his plea to be heard was met with the cursory dismissal: "No, you're just too much of an arsehole to live with. Keith and I have got something going." For Brian this rejection entailed a complete collapse of morale, and faced with what he felt to be the onset of another breakdown, he admitted himself to the Priory Clinic in Roehampton on March 9 1967, where he was visited by his friend, Nicholas Fitzgerald. Nicholas has told us of his finding Brian dressed in a gold dressing gown, deeply depressed and unwilling to discuss the traumatised events leading to his collapse.

Built in 1811 as a private residence set in 4,000 acres, the Priory became a psychiatric hospital in the 1870s. Brian was no stranger to this palatial edifice situated on the borders of Kew and Richmond, and its tolerant but disciplined regime was to prove instrumental to his nervous recovery on a number of occasions. The pristine magnolia-walled bedroom he occupied, frugal in furnishings, but spartanly comfortable, provided a sympathetic detox precinct for the two weeks preceding the upcoming Rolling Stones European tour. Although Brian was nervously charred, psychologically demeaned and confidence-undermined, it was imperative if he was to keep is place in the band, that he should undertake the tour. And despite his only being twenty-five, and adulated to the point of receiving thousands of fan letters each month, Brian's private life had proved a continuous disaster. Few of his fans would have recognised the fragmented, jittery and alienated Brian who lay exhausted in his monastic room at the Priory. His dependencies were arguably curable, and there is every reason to believe that by the end of his life Brian was no longer doing drugs, but his ravaged psychic interior was altogether more damaged. All of his life Brian had assimilated rejection. His extreme sensitivity, and his tendency towards a narcissistic form of self-worship made rejection insupportably hard for him to carry. Anita Pallenberg's chic sixties attractiveness, and the magnitude generated by her force of personality, had made her appear to Brian his ideal counterpart. Brian had been envied for what appeared to outsiders the perfect relationship. Not only had he suffered a brutal form of rejection, but Brian had lost Anita to someone who featured large on his map of paranoid misgivings. Brian felt humiliated, and unable to voice his raw sense of anger within the band's political infrastructure, he turned the aggression in on himself.

In terms of nervous strain the tour on which Brian embarked proved to be one of the ugliest in the band's history. Taking in nine European countries, they and their entourage were subjected to methodical baggage and body searches whenever they passed through customs. The band's association with drugs was now common knowledge to the international police. Brian, like his colleagues, was often stripped naked in the rigorous search carried out by Customs for illicit substances. At the end of their exhaustive tour, and in the wake of audience riots wherever they played, the Rolling Stones performed a historic concert behind the Iron Curtain in Warsaw. Outside the chosen venue, the Palace of Culture, the police in an attempt to suppress an insurgent youth turned high-pressure water hoses on the crowd, before unleashing Dobermans and tear-gas on an uproarious youth. Given that Brian was precariously skirting the edges of mental collapse, these sordid incidents were the last form of pressures to which he should have been exposed.

Brian's education, together with his introverted character, was such that he would rarely discuss his personal problems with friends. His needs when they were made manifest were invariably to do with practicalities, and so internal scars were largely left unhealed, and unaddressed by constructive discourse. Brian attempted to conceal his emotional breakage, and back at Courtfield Road he resumed his old self-destructive habits.

Brian's friend, Christopher Gibbs, has given us a picture of the debris and chaos that ensued at Courtfield Road, as an impractical and alcohol-dependent Brian attempted not only to exorcise Pallenberg's demonic aura, but also to reintegrate the threads of his shattered life. "He was living in complete chaos," Gibbs tells us. "He had hundreds of beautiful clothes, but these were left lying about all over the floor, either burnt or covered in food... There were dozens of instruments that were smashed and hadn't been repaired; they were scattered everywhere. It was a terrible mess, but it was the same wherever he went... He didn't live like normal people. He didn't go to bed at night and get up in the morning, he got up when he felt like it and went to bed when he felt like it. It didn't have anything to do with when the buses were running, or the banks were open or even if there was any daylight. Everyone had to revolve around him. He would arrive at a restaurant just as it was closing with eight or ten people in it, at about 12.45, and he would be surprised when they had nothing on the menu and he would make a fuss about it."

Brian's inability to differentiate between day and night, and his failure to impose a disciplined structure on his life suggests an individual radically divorced from reality. Brian's psychiatrist had postulated that a prison sentence could result in a psychotic breakdown on the part of his patient, and a complete departure from reality. That Brian lived on the threshold of psychosis seems to have been established beyond doubt, and that this condition was aggravated by the consumption of drugs and alcohol seems further to have contributed to his state of disordered mental health. In terms of the decadent tradition, we can notably enlist the person of Count Eric Stenbock as analogous to Brian's situation of living at a remove from reality.

Stenbock's wealth, opium habit and alcoholism all encouraged him to sever ties with the practical world. He finally withdrew into a private, drug-inspired microcosm, out of which he wrote the vampire stories collected in *Studies In Death* (1894). Increasingly isolated and socially outlawed for his homosexuality, Stenbock had made for him a life-size doll, in the form of an attractive youth, who he addressed as "le petit comte". According to Stenbock's biographer John Adlard, the Count on his travels "had to be escorted, and with him went a dog, a monkey and a life-size doll. He was convinced that the doll was his son and referred to him as 'le petit comte'. Every day it had to be brought to him; when it was not there he would ask for news of its health. The Stenbocks believed that a dishonest monk – or perhaps a Jesuit – had extorted large sums of money from him under the pretence of paying for the education of 'le petit comte'."

Stenbock's love of ostentatiously sumptuous clothes – he opened the door to the artist Simeon Solomon dressed in a scarlet silk gown motifed with gold dragons – was just one aspect of life he shared in common with Brian Jones. Both men were eminently foppish, disregarded conventions, took refuge in stimulants to help cushion them from reality, and generally lived outside the law. Stenbock's wealth and title, together with the absence of narcotics laws pertaining to opium and hashish in the London of the 1890s, allowed him to smoke without fear of police interference. Unlike Wilde, the equally available Stenbock seems to have been successful in screening his homosexuality from the threat of prosecution. He lived the pampered hedonistic life of the dilettante whose eccentricities are accounted for by a private inheritance. Brian's problem in 1960s London was that the parameters of his private life were constantly being invaded and made public, by virtue of his being a member of the Rolling Stones. Unlike Stenbock, the drugs he took by way of experimentation were illegal, and he was to pay a heavy price in terms of persecution by the authorities for his use of illicit drugs. Stenbock was left to pursue his spectrum of bizarre idiosyncrasies to the ruin of his health, while Brian as a public image was on two occasions brought to justice.

In this state of ill health, Brian endeavoured to find a creative resonance in his life, and undertook an ambitious project in completing the scoring of the German avant-garde film, *Mord Und Totschlag* ("A Degree Of Murder"), which ironically starred Anita Pallenberg. For Brian the opportunity presented a chance to prove his musicianship independent of the Rolling Stones. His knowledge of diverse instruments, and his intuitive flair for mood colouring were to prove the ideal criteria for the project in hand. Working at home with two small tape machines, Brian's imagination excelled at creating a lyrical score. The work became his obsession, and for once in his life he showed a discipline in applying himself to his task which had been absent from his recent recording sessions with the Rolling Stones. Enlisting the likes of Jimmy Page on guitar, and Nicky Hopkins on piano, Brian was to embellish the studio score with instruments as diverse as flute, sitar, banjo, autoharp and jazz piano. The resulting aural mosaic was an inspired success, with Brian turning a project that could have been merely eccentric into a genuinely admired art form. He had proved that left to his own devices and removed from the inhibiting sense of inferiority that he felt in the presence of Jagger and Richards, his creative expression remained untarnished. The film's director Volker Schlöndorff has said of Brian's musical abilities: "It wasn't just that his music was special, it was that the score was so spontaneous and vital. Only Brian could have done it. He had a tremendous feeling for the lyrical parts and knew perfectly the recording and mixing techniques to achieve the best sound."

That Brian was the member of the Rolling Stones most admired by other musicians for his virtuosic abilities as an original colourist was something sadly lost on his increasing lack of self-esteem. Jagger and Richards had conspired to make Brian feel like an impotent casualty in the studio, and he in turn had begun to believe in his inadequacy. Terrified of being rejected by the band, he would arrive at the session too inebriated to play, and so fulfil the group's expectations that he was redundant to their needs. The Stones's producer Jimmy Miller has said of Brian's quandary within group politics: "In his last eighteen months with the group, Brian was plagued with personal problems, and his musical differences with the rest of the group were increasingly apparent. He was entirely a musician and never quite adapted to the commercial image aspects of being a Stone... when the sessions (*Beggar's Banquet*) first started, Brian came up to me and said he didn't think he would be able to contribute much. When we began working he really got into it and started to get excited. Then he came up to me and apologised for having had any doubts at the beginning."

Brian's weird mood oscillations depended greatly on the theme of self-belief. In a depressed state, and Brian seemed unwilling to confront his inner demons without resorting to drugs, he relied on Tuinols and Mandrax to prop up his negative feelings about himself. If Brian had been willing to confront his obsessions with the help of Jungian or archetypal psychology, and without the use of pharmaceuticals, some attempt at healing may have taken place. As it was, Brian's negative moods spiralled into pockets of increasing psychic nihilism, as he attacked his depression with both prescription and non-prescription drugs. Like so many sixties people he relied on the user-friendly Valium (Diazepam), one of the Benzodiazepine family of sedatives, to help cope with anxiety problems.

In an effort to free himself of his loneliness, Brian moved a new blonde devotee, Suki Potier, into Courtfield Road, in the hope of finding in her looks a substitute for Pallenberg. Brian continued to pursue the latter and to be brutally rebuffed by her lack of sympathy for his person. It was during this transitional phase in his confused personal relations that Brian was stopped in his tracks by the first of his drug busts. Raided by Scotland Yard at the instigation of an informer, only weeks after Jagger and Richards had been busted at Redlands, DS Norman Pilcher of Scotland Yard found himself in a flat in which a huge Nazi flag was draped over an armchair. After a brief search Brian, whose only company in the flat was the Polish aristocrat, Prince Stanislaus, was – together with his friend – charged with the unlawful possession of dangerous drugs and ordered to appear at Marlborough Street Magistrates Court the following day. Brian, who was still suffering the post-traumatic effects of shock after his betrayal in Morocco, was at his most vulnerable at the time of the raid. The breakdown he had undergone as a consequence of losing the security provided by his relationship, had turned into an unopposed landslide of terror, as he was brought chillingly face to face with the prospects of imprisonment. Brian was understandably unhinged by the experience. He had been confronted by a form of reality which he not only despised, but one which was empowered to take away his liberty. The night he spent in the cells was coloured by the threats of warders who were awaiting the chance to cut his hair, as well as brutalised by the insulting shrieks of adjoining prisoners who lost no opportunity in declaring Brian a faggot and a poof.

Everything in Brian's life seemed to have collapsed, and he lacked sufficient direction in himself to stand back and review things objectively. Instead, his paranoia quickly escalated into a persecution mania. Back at his flat he became obsessed with the idea that his telephone was bugged, and he would periodically pick up the receiver and scream abuse into the mouth-piece. Somebody had clearly resolved on the idea of spooking Brian, and pushing him beyond limits. He grew suspicious of stationary cars parked outside in the street, and conducted an impromptu press conference from his balcony, claiming that his private life was being mercilessly invaded by the authorities. His nervous deterioration was visible in his ravaged features. He had grown to be like that other blonde degenerate, Marilyn Monroe, whose symptoms of inner turmoil were steadily written into her deconstructing beauty. Brian's latent potential for hysteria was unleashed to the full by the menacing events that crowded into his life in the first half of 1967. Lacking the more resilient and hardened sensibilities of his colleagues Jagger and Richards, Brian's reaction to crisis was the feminine one of emotional breakdown. Whereas Keith Richards, placed in the cells overnight requested a pen and paper, and drew up his chair in the morning to face the light admitted from a high window, Brian was signally broken by the experience, and never fully recovered.

For Oscar Wilde, as another aesthete faced with the appalling depersonalisation of individual needs which prison brought, it was also the noisome stench of primitive latrines, the deliberately offensive food and the lack of sympathetic discourse which so offended. Unlike Wilde, Brian was spared a prison sentence, but in his imagination he must have conceived of the worst form of claustrophobic confinement and personal degradation while awaiting the outcome of this trial. In one of his letters from prison Wilde had written: "I let myself be lured into long spells of senseless and sensual ease. I amused myself with being a flâneur, a dandy, a man of fashion. I surrounded myself with the smaller natures and the meaner minds. I became a spendthrift of my own genius... Tired of being on the heights I deliberately went to the depths... I grew careless." And to another correspondent Wilde confessed: "It is the sin of pride which has always destroyed men. I had risen too high, and I fell sprawling in the mire."

Brian Jones had also risen too high in the pantheon of pop demi-gods who hijacked the cultural attention of a sixties youth. Success invariably leads to a corresponding fall, and the anti-authoritarianism inherent in Brian's adulated bisexual stance was one which served as an irritant to the Establishment. Brian was very clearly the brains at work in the Rolling Stones, and if the latter were to be silenced, then he was the obvious target to hit. And in the prosecution of Jagger, Richards and Brian Jones, the authorities succeeded in putting the group's future in serious jeopardy. For a brief period in 1967 it looked as if the Rolling Stones would, if prosecution proved successful, cease to exist as a unit.

In the middle of Brian's catastrophic personal collapse, the pop ethos was in the summer of 1967 to celebrate the release of the Beatles's *Sgt. Pepper's Lonely Hearts Club Band.* Fusing the advent of flower power with a musical dynamic inspired by the visionary experiences attendant on taking LSD, the Beatles had succeeded in manufacturing the perfect record to match the times. With intuitive foresight they had created the album of the decade, and succeeded in making psychedelia into a popular art form.

As a distraction from his manifold problems and impending court case, Brian flew to America to attend the Monterey International Pop Festival, ostensibly to introduce his friend Jimi Hendrix on stage. Dressed in a gold and pink fringed cloak, embellished with a water-fall of sparkling costume jewellery, Brian spent three days at the liberated hippie festival, reportedly tripping on acid, and discussing his visions with the resident hierarchy grouped around campfires. In the regalia of a drag queen and with his hair dyed gold, Brian resembled the ultimate transgender archetype created by his generation. Brian had never appeared quite so radically divorced from reality, as he wandered amongst the crowds as the unofficial Queen of Ceremonies, or perhaps as a drug-addled Acid King.

On his return to London Brian, who was paranoid that his Courtfield Road flat was under police scrutiny, decided to move with Suki and a minder into a suite of rooms in the Royal Gardens Hotel in Kensington. The Rolling Stones organisation installed Brian

Palastanga as minder for Brian, a character whose criminal behaviour was to extend to the theft of two of Brian's valuable cameras, before being removed from his position as chauffeur. According to reports Brian was under severe mental stress at the time, smoked large quantities of hashish and regularly threatened suicide. His attempts to dissipate his psychological crises through the medium of alcohol were ineffectual, and Brian was again presumed to be swimming perilously close to breakdown. It was in this drug-imploded and peculiarly vulnerable state that Brian intermittently attended sessions at Olympic Studios for the recording of the Rolling Stones's answer to the psychedelic phenomenon: *Their Satanic Majesties Request.* Once again Brian withdrew from playing guitar in the sessions, and acted as a sensitive colourist, dubbing a range of exotic instruments onto basic rock and roll tracks given an overtly psychedelic sound. Brian's maverick role of exotic improviser was the best compromise he could offer under personally harrowing circumstances. Brian supplied phrases of mellotron, Indian drums, flutes, recorder, sitar and orchestral harp to the album's flagrant attempt to match the Beatles's innovative psychedelic measures on *Sgt. Pepper's Lonely Hearts Club Band.* No matter that Brian was basically disapproving of the Rolling Stones's singular excursion into psychedelia, his contributions to the album were singled out by reviewers as comprising the record's merit. Brian's musicianship was considered to be the one redemptive quality of a work which was otherwise reviewed as a mis-assessed attempt to rival the Beatles's altogether superior project. Brian, who had issued grave warnings to his colleagues about the possibly disastrous consequences of deserting their R&B roots, had been proved right by his prophetic warnings. His constantly losing fight to have the Rolling Stones subscribe to a rockier rhythm and blues format, one which best featured Jagger's negroid vocals and the band's punchier and controversial stage presence, had been basically overridden in the face of studio refinement.

Brian's criticisms, even though they were to be heeded on the recording of the band's next album *Beggar's Banquet,* were at the time disregarded. Brian's level of nervous exhaustion was such that he had to be propped up on a pile of cushions during the sessions for *Their Satanic Majesties Request,* from the support of which he courageously continued to add baroque flourishes to the music. Brian had rightly refused to capitulate his place in the band, no matter his obvious state of ill-health, and once again had succeeded in pulling himself back from the edge of breakdown. His holding up to work pressures was both felicitous and timely, and put pay to rumours that his redundancy within the Stones was imminent.

If nothing else, Brian was to be freed of the rigorous debilitation that comes of touring by what was to prove a two-year interlude in the band's hectic diary of live dates. Chauffeur-driven in his Silver Cloud Rolls Royce back and forth from the studio, his frayed nervous state rendered him a semi-invalid. On one occasion Brian was to turn back from a session as he was convinced that the studio was dense with giant black beetles, while on another excursion to Olympic he grew terrified of being suffocated by swarms of exotic butterflies. Brian's apprehension of a threatening psychic menagerie was doubtless in part caused by his use of hallucinogenic drugs. The damage done to his mind by a surfeit of pharmaceuticals mirrored the disturbing addictions suffered by Edgar Allan Poe, Charles Baudelaire and Count Eric Stenbock, all of whom re-opened inner wounds by seeking respite in drugs. It was Baudelaire who confided in his *Intimate Journals*: "Even in childhood I felt two conflicting sensations in my heart: the horror of life and the ecstasy of life. That, indeed, was the mark of a bored neurotic."

Brian on drugs would see monsters in his flat, and hear satanic voices issuing from domestic appliances. And given that he was in his own mind living at the heart of a conspiracy to remove him from his place in the Rolling Stones, his need to make himself additionally vulnerable in this way suggests a degree of self-hatred amounting to masochism. Brian's masochistic tendencies, rooted in his unhappy childhood, would have been greatly encouraged by his relationship with Anita Pallenberg, in which he was often the submissively willing victim, nonetheless seething with rage at his sadistic partner.

Faced with the imminent prospect of his trial for being in unlawful possession of drugs, Brian skirted the edges of nervous disintegration. He and Suki moved into a new flat at number 17, Chesham Street, in London's Belgravia, an attempt on Brian's part not only to exorcise old demons, but also to elude harassing police surveillance. When Brian appeared in court on 30 October at Inner London Sessions, he was dressed in a dark grey pinstriped suit, a white shirt with the then fashionable long pointed collar and a cobalt coloured polka-dot tie. Brian's eminent QC, James Comyn, pleaded that the pressures attendant on being a pop star had contributed to

Brian's experimenting with soft drugs, and promised that Brian would never touch cannabis again. Brian's psychiatrist, Dr. Henry, argued that a prison sentence "would completely destroy (Brian's)' mental health, he would go into a psychotic depression, he might even attempt to injure himself". Brian, in a convincingly repentant mood, spoke from the witness box of drugs as having "only brought me trouble and disrupted my career, and I hope this will be an example to anyone who is tempted to try them."

Despite the insubstantial nature of the charges, and an eloquent appeal from Brian's counsel for mitigating circumstances, Brian was sentenced to nine months, and was led away in handcuffs, to be transported to Wormwood Scrubs. Even though Brian was to be released the following day on bail on medical grounds to await appeal in December, the experience left his nerves shattered. His confrontation with a brutally punitive legal system, and the claustrophobia-inducing horror of facing the interior of a grey prison van, had left him in constant tears and subject to excruciating asthmatic attacks.

In the account of his humiliation and degradation suffered in prison, Oscar Wilde wrote in *De Profundis* of the wounding insults he had received in the course of being transferred from London to Reading jail. Wilde writes: "Of all possible objects I was the most grotesque. When people saw me they laughed. Each train as it came up swelled the audience. Nothing could exceed their amusement. That was, of course, before they knew who I was. As soon as they had been informed they laughed still more. For half an hour I stood there in the grey November rain surrounded by a jeering mob." Wilde goes on to tell us: "For a year after that was done to me I wept every day at the same hour and for the same space of time. That is not such a tragic thing as possibly it sounds to you. To those who are in prison tears are part of every day's experience. A day in prison on which one does not weep is a day on which one's heart is hard, not a day on which one's heart is happy."

Brian would no doubt have sympathised with Wilde's confessional account of the travesties of justice which left the poet a broken pariah on his release from prison in 1897. When it came to Brian's appeal in December, he was to win advantage over Wilde in that psychological evaluation was considered a justifiable form of evidence. It was the appeal to Brian's being "in an extremely precarious state of emotional adjustment" which was to lead to his sentence being repealed. Lord Chief Justice Parker was in agreement with the psychiatric reports prepared on Brian, and the latter's nine-month sentence was set aside on the condition that Brian continued to have psychiatric treatment. He was in addition fined £1,000 and put on probation for a period of three years.

On the advice of Dr. Flood Brian, who had been admitted to the Priory Clinic following another crisis admission, was advised to take a holiday. In need of relaxation after the months of high anxiety preceding his appeal, a nervously shaky Brian flew out to Ceylon, with Linda Keith as his companion. But any vestiges of stability returning to Brian's dissipated lifestyle were shattered in March 1968, when he returned home to his Chesham Street address to find the door had been demolished by a police contingent led by the redoubtably antagonistic DS Pilcher, under the pretext of searching the property for drugs. Within weeks, Brian's temporary girlfriend Linda Keith was to overdose and to be found naked on the bed in the same apartment, and the resulting press sensation, "Stone Girl Naked In Drug Drama", was to send shock waves of acute paranoia through Brian's unhinged mind. He rightly felt himself to be under intense police scrutiny, and in his own way he may well have owned to Meister Eckhart's telescoped metaphor: "The eye with which I see God is the eye with which he sees me". For Brian, DS Pilcher's features must have stuck in his mind like an omnipresent adversary, a craggy cliff-face obtruding into his consciousness, and terrifying him with unspoken threat. It was enough to drive anyone mad, and for Brian, who was living perilously on the edge of psychotic disturbance, Pilcher's infiltrating presence was aimed at encouraging suicide in the distressed musician.

In his efforts to avoid attention Brian adopted a nomadic form of life, and after having been evicted from his Chesham Street address, took refuge in a series of West End hotels, before going as far abroad as Sussex, Kent and Cornwall in the effort to find the anonymity that he was denied in London. It was on one of his rural itineraries conducted in a blue Rolls Royce that Brian was to fall in love with his future home, Cotchford Farm, the former residence of the writer A.A. Milne. Dressed in a white fur coat and a plum-coloured Ascot hat Brian, reclining in the rear of his chauffeur-driven limousine, resembled a youthfully debauched Emperor, as he looked out at the diamond-frosted winter landscape. An Emperor bound for sacrificial death.

Brian's only work with the Rolling Stones was to lay down his guitar track for the single "Jumping Jack Flash", the song which was to restore the group to the premier chart position in the summer of 1968. After the tepid critical response evoked by the band's excursion into quasi-psychedelia on *Their Satanic Majesties Request*, Brian's advice was to prove instrumental to the Stones's decision to return to their more primitive R&B roots on the album's successor *Beggar's Banquet*. In still another attempt to find privacy, Brian moved into a third floor rented flat in Royal Avenue House, King's Road, an address which facilitated his addiction to clothing purchases in the galaxy of boutiques which flourished along Chelsea's King's Road.

But a change of address brought no respite from the series of catastrophes attendant on Brian's life. On 21 May 1968, at about 7.20 a.m., he was awoken by the noise of the police breaking down his door for entry. In what was undoubtedly a set-up, the police procured a ball of blue wool from a bureau drawer, and claimed to have found a piece of cannabis or Indian hemp concealed in it. If, as has been pertinently suggested, the drug had been planted there by somebody in the Stones's organisation, who had then informed the police, then this would account for the rapid success of the search. Brian disowned all knowledge of the substance, and pointed to the fact that he was temporarily renting a furnished flat, and had no knowledge of the apartment's contents. Brian's publicist, Les Perrin, who was suspected of acting as informer in this incident, later denied involvement in the bust and claimed: "I remain convinced that Brian was innocent of that second bust. I phoned Brian from Chichester to tell him that a friend of mine at the newspaper had told me that he was going to be busted."

Brian was summarily taken in a tremulous state to Chelsea police station, where he was formally charged, before appearing that afternoon at Marlborough Street Magistrates Court. Charged with unlawful possession of cannabis, he was released on £2,000 bail pending trial before the Inner London sessions.

Life had grown to be dangerously, terrifyingly bad for Brian. What should have been years of enviable, youthful, heady success with an internationally acclaimed pop band, who had acquired wealth and fame, had devolved in Brian's case to a drug-cocktailed debacle in which he fought to maintain sanity. Whatever Brian was struggling to achieve at this point of his career seems to have had very little to do with music. All of his energies were directed at dealing with profound inner crises, and the savage mood swings to which he was subject suggest that in 1968 Brian should have been hospitalised. On impulse he had begun to purchase double-decker buses, a tram and a horse-drawn charabanc, as well as a Battersea Park Fun Fair roundabout called "The Waltzer".

Brian was once again admitted to the Priory Nursing Home, complaining of depression and attendant hallucinations. He was manifestly dysfunctional as a creative artist, and imbued with a sense of self-hatred which revealed itself in his sexual relations as a refusal to make love to women on the grounds that he would be defiling them. When one afternoon in May, 1968, Brian invited his casual girlfriend, Debby Scott, to visit him at his room in the Imperial Hotel, London, she found him hostilely cold and unwilling to speak. After a time Brian awkwardly directed her towards the door, saying: "Don't make me degrade you."

Debby had been a regular visitor to Brian's King's Road flat, and was there the afternoon before he was busted, and he retained misgivings about her as a possible informer. They had taken acid together, and LSD seems always in Brian to have provoked a deep-seated misogyny. Brian's estranged and deranged life at this time resembled the protagonist of Charles Baudelaire's poem "Spleen", in which a ruined "King of the rain country" lists complaints about the impossibility of stimulating his jaded senses. Brian needed orgies, lesbianism to which he was a spectator, and gay sex to inspire his own depleted libido. His frazzled senses no longer connected with reality. Brian was temporarily put under the watchful eye of the minder he most feared, Tom Keylock, at Keith Richards's vacant Redlands residence, and a crude method of detox was enforced by the authoritarian Keylock. Brian had every reason to dislike a man who had been an accomplice to the Moroccan plot in which he had lost Anita Pallenberg to Keith Richards, and Brian anyhow sensed in Keylock a close resemblance to his father's militant disposition. Tom Keylock was the last person with whom Brian should have been shut up in his hallucinatory mental state.

Marianne Faithfull has reported an incident which occurred at Redlands when, attempting to repair the fissure in the band which existed between Brian and Jagger, she invited them both to dinner at Redlands. A verbal and then physical fight ensued between Jones and Jagger, which resulted in Brian narrowly missing stabbing Jagger with a carving knife, before running outside with the intention of killing himself by jumping into the turbid, twenty feet deep moat. Jagger was apparently forced to jump in and physically man-haul Jones to safety, the two embattled antagonists continuing to thrash and flail in the muddy water.

This reported incident serves not only as a commentary on Brian's mental condition, but on how deep a resentment he had come to nurture for Jagger's progressive ascendancy to spokesman and recognised leader of the Rolling Stones. Although friction was to slow-burn for another year before Brian was forced out of the Stones, this ugly incident at Redlands was to permanently discredit his character in a group who had grown impatient with carrying a nervous casualty.

Replacing a dependency on eclectic drugs with an insatiable reliance on alcohol, Brian succeeded in cushioning himself from reality in the immediate run-up to his second trial on 24 September. Once again psychiatric reports were to play a crucial role in Brian's acquittal, and Dr. Flood's trenchant testimony, "If I put a reefer cigarette by this young man he would run a mile", was to prove persuasive in having charges dropped. Despite the jury finding Brian guilty, Chairman Reginald Seaton had reason to suspect little more than circumstantial evidence on the part of the police, and refused to entertain the idea of a prison sentence for the defendant. Operating on the laws of plain common sense, Seaton was to look favourably on Brian's situation, and overruled the jury. "I think this was a lapse," he stated, "and I don't want to interfere with the probation order that applies to this man. I am going to fine you according to your means. You must keep clear of this stuff. You really must watch your step. You will be fined fifty pounds with one hundred guineas costs. For goodness sake, don't get into trouble again or you really will be in serious trouble."

Chairman Seaton's sympathetic understanding of Brian's predicament as a pop star subjected to inordinate public pressures, and as someone struggling with a habit, placed a redemptive note on judicial proceedings. An elated Brian left court determined to reanimate his dormant creative faculty, but also shadowed by his evident exclusion from a band he had worked so hard to found. His life was in ruins no matter his acquittal, and for the remaining year left to him he was to stare long and hard at the residual damage of his tragic youth.

FOUR: **NO EXPECTATIONS**

"A woman should wear her perfume wherever she wants to be kissed."

—Coco Chanel

Brian's fascination with Morocco as a country ideally suited to the fluent interchange between his inner and outer worlds, was to remain constant throughout the period of deep stress associated with his two trials.

Prior to returning to Morocco, after his second trial, with the specific purpose of recording the legendary Jajoukan musicians, Brian had on a slightly earlier visit given evidence of the violent mania which possessed him on occasions. According to Brian's friend, the antiquarian, Christopher Gibbs, who had accompanied Brian and Suki on their brief visit to Tangier, he was resting in his room one evening when Brian rushed in and began hysterically to confess that he had beaten Suki senseless. According to Gibbs, "He was really hysterical. So I went with him to his room and the whole place was a mess. Smashed mirrors, smashed glass, smashed everything, and Suki was lying on the bed, unconscious and bleeding... He had given her the most terrible beating for one reason or another... I managed to get a doctor and an ambulance and they turned up with Suki still unconscious, while Brian was pretending he had nothing whatsoever to do with it."

What is telling in the situations where Brian manifested symptoms of manic violence is that the women whom he beat seldom rejected him as a consequence of his unpredictable bouts of aggression. Brian never seems to have become violent with men, and

---

the objects of his assault were invariably women and domestic furnishings. To break a room up and leave somebody seriously injured on the bed is a dangerous game, and clearly the pathological violence of Brian's assaults could have led to murder. Brian's sense of detachment from his acts of aggression was almost pathological, and points back to the chilling emotional climate in which he was raised. His absence of responsibility for his actions was of course condoned in his mind by his self-belief in his elevated status as an artist. Brian's conviction of the extraordinariness attached to the creative sensibility differed little from Oscar Wilde's theory that anything and everything is morally pardonable in the name of art.

These vicious scenes in which Brian physically recriminated against women seem to have had their origins in his deep-rooted sexual confusion. According to Nicholas Fitzgerald in his account of Brian's bisexual polarities, Brian was to confess: "I was touched up once at school by an older boy. It was in the shower after a rugby match. It was a bit of a violent assault and it might have had some subconscious effect on me. Maybe it made me go around laying as many girls as I could just to prove I wasn't gay. But now I don't think it matters. All I know is that I don't like sleeping alone and I don't see much difference sleeping with a boy or a girl. Both can be cuddly."

Subsequent to Brian's unguarded admissions to Nicholas Fitzgerald about his sexual preferences, the two dropped acid in Brian's Monterey hotel bedroom, and went to bed together. Nicholas tells us: "Brian helped me into bed. I lay in bed for hours with his arm over me. I guess the LSD had kicked in." Again, what we are informed of here is an act of tender caring infused with homo-eroticism, a very different ideal to the repeated beatings and cruelty that Brian meted out to Anita Pallenberg and Suki Potier. Brian clearly felt hugely threatened in his sexual relations with women, and was also reluctant to form the commitments that may come of relation-ships. Nicholas Fitzgerald is our source for Brian's apparent misogyny. In conversation with his friend, Brian was to tell Nicholas: "...I hate commitments. You know, the kind of commitments that can tie you down to a little house hung about with babies' diapers. God, that would kill me – kill my soul anyway – if I've got one. No, I don't think I could ever get married."

In the immediate elation following his court release, Brian returned to Morocco, again accompanied by Suki, and this time with the sound engineer George Chikiantz making up their small party. Brian's intention was to record the native Jajoukan musicians, and then to dub the tapes either with black music or contributions by the Rolling Stones. The concept was based within the framework of quirky ideas at which Brian excelled, and which formed so much of the intuitive genius that he was to bring to mid-sixties pop music. Brian was determined to record the Jajouka's Pan Rites, and his resolve to do so was another example of how well he could discipline himself to complete projects independent of the Stones. As with his scoring the soundtrack for *A Degree Of Murder*, he showed a genuinely inspired empathy for his subject, no matter how short-lived.

Brian and his party set off to the remote mountainous village of Jajouka, located in the Ahl-Sarif province of Morocco to the south-west of Tangier. Dressed in his colourful Ikat robes, and with his highlighted blond hair having the village inhabitants assume they had met an apotheosis, he and his group arrived at sundown. They sat on a hillside smoking hashish and taking in the ceremonially guarded rites of the Pan Festival. By all accounts Brian, no matter the oddity of his appearance to the indigenous villagers, was well received by the Jajoukans. His inquisitiveness about matters relating to ethnic music, and his uncanny ability to learn immediately how to play a Jajoukan pipe quickly endeared him to the natives. Brian, who conceived of himself as representing the sacrificial goat eaten at a great feast in his honour, left an indelible mark on a community who had rarely seen Europeans. The writer, Brion Gysin, who was also in attendance over the two days of the Pan Rites, has left this anecdotal sketch of the culminatory banquet: "It was getting to be time to eat," Gysin writes, "and suddenly two of the musicians came along with a snow-white goat. The goat disappeared off into the shadows with two musicians, one of whom was holding a long knife which Brian suddenly caught the glitter of, and he started to get up, making a funny noise, and he said: 'That's me!' And everybody picked up on it right at once and said: 'Yeah, right, it looks just like you.' It was perfectly true, he had this fringe of blond hair hanging right in front of his eyes, and we said: 'Of course that's you!' Then about twenty minutes later we were eating this goat's liver on shish kebab sticks."

Brian's focused energies sustained him over the necessary two days of recording. Loving music as he did, his sense of integrated self was never more apparent than when fully engaged with his creative dynamic. He was the first of the sixties musicians to express a concern with ethnic music. While his tapes were rejected by the Rolling Stones's hierarchy, the fruits of his Moroccan labours were to appear posthumously under the title of *Brian Jones Presents The Pipes Of Pan At Jajouka*, on Rolling Stones Records in 1971.

Back at the Hotel Minzah, after having undertaken his successful recordings of the Jajoukan pipes, Brian's behaviour switched to an anti-social, masochistically destructive mode of expression. He stood on his hotel balcony stoned, and yelled abuse at passers-by in the street. It was still another instance of Brian's dramatic mood swings, and his aggressive behaviour may have arisen from the paranoid effects of having smoked an excess of marijuana. Brian's seeming inability to sustain an emotional constant in his relations with others was a behavioural characteristic which mirrored his inner state of psychic disintegration. But clearly he was also possessed of a range of endearing and sensitive qualities which had friends remain loyal, and more than that, willing to offer assistance in times of crisis. The confusion in how he perceived himself, stemmed largely from his belief that he was attractive to people because he was a member of the Rolling Stones. Yet on the contrary, Brian seems to have formed secure friendships with those who respected his fine and easily dented sensitivity.

Back in London Brian continued to attend sessions for the *Beggar's Banquet* album which the Rolling Stones were recording at Olympic Studios. But according to the Stones's engineer George Chikiantz, Jagger and Richards were unremittingly hard on Brian's attenuated nerves, and endlessly discouraged his attempts to contribute to the new material. In *One Plus One*, Jean-Luc Godard's cinematic document of the recording of *Beggar's Banquet*'s key track "Sympathy For The Devil", Brian's alienation and dissociation are cruelly highlighted. Chikiantz has recalled the scenes of Brian's victimisation as: "It was a bit much the way they were going on at him. But Brian was no longer capable of fulfilling a real function in the group. It was difficult to contact him, like talking to a shadow. He just wasn't there, inside of his body. The saddest thing was to watch Brian spend three and a half hours trying to put a reed into a saxophone and nobody could stop him. We had to wait until he got thirsty and give him another Mandrax to send him to sleep."

Somehow Chikiantz's inconsideration is consistent with the whole insensitive policy applied to a broken individual by his so-called colleagues. Rather than just give Brian another Mandrax to sedate him, did nobody consider that a modicum of sympathy and perhaps three months recuperation in a clinic would have been beneficial to helping Brian recover his equanimity after the series of shocks attendant on the circumstances of his two arrests? Brian seems to have been the defenceless victim of those who delight in taking advantage of vulnerability. There are always individuals who voyeuristically derive pleasure in feeding an alcoholic drinks, or an addict drugs. In Brian's circle there seems to have been no lack of persons willing to encourage his excesses with the morbid fascination of spectators eager to view the extremes of self-destruction.

The spectacle of an educated, refined person becoming an object of disdain and mockery in the studio was an ugly one. However ineffectual as a musician Brian may have appeared in this difficult phase, and however intolerable his untogetherness was to musicians looking to consolidate their professionalism, he was nonetheless not only their founder member, but also their brains. Brian's articulacy and ability to formulate challengingly cogent statements about music were always with him, no matter the circumstances of his health. Interviewed in the mid-sixties about his experimental competence with harmonica, he was to crystallise his views with a clarity that his other band members lacked. He was to say of the harmonica: "They're not musical instruments really in the proper sense of the word. The secret of playing this little harmonica and getting our sort of sound is bending the notes. It's a completely different method of playing a harmonica. You don't play the notes straight, you have to bend them to get this whining sound. In actual fact, they're not chromatic at all. You don't even have the eight straight notes of the octave, you have to make something yourself and this you do by bending, as well. I couldn't possibly give anybody any tips on playing the harmonica. It's just a matter of getting to know the feel of it. You mess about with the harmonica for a few months and all of a sudden you can get this sound. I don't even know how to do it myself. It's done in the throat. You alter the volume of your throat, you know."

This articulate statement by a virtuoso bluesman, with its valuable blend of modesty and creative insight, is hardly the inchoate rambling of a dysfunctional person. There's an intimate and sharing confidence to all of Brian's interview statements which profess both high intelligence and a certain measure of creative humility. If Brian's defence mechanism was to adopt a mode of assumed arrogance in public, then his thoughts about his work are modest and illuminatingly constructive. His friend, Ronni Money, has recalled Brian's willingness to be open to all influences of music, and out of a sense of inquisitive eclecticism to compound diverse styles into his method of playing. Money remembers: "...the beautiful thing about Brian was that he didn't think he was the only person. He knew that there were corners of the world, villages in outer Siberia where somebody was probably sitting down and playing better than him and would never be heard. In fact, he said that to me – not with the intention of exploiting them, but with the intention of learning from them."

Brian's written contribution to the text prepared by himself and Brion Gysin to accompany their experiment in recording the Jajoukan musicians contained the following highly perceptive insight on Brian's part. In defence of the sometimes inaudible vocal parts of the tapes Brian wrote: "We apologise for the virtual inaudibility of the lead singer during the chanting of the women, but she and others are singing not to an audience of mortals but rather they are chanting an incantation to those on another plane, and while we were recording her she hid her beautiful voice behind the drum she was playing. It was not for our ears."

This sensitive elucidation by Brian as to the gnosis contained within the music, shows how deeply he entered into the trance-like states inspired by the Pan Rites. One of the young villagers, Bachir Attar, was years later to recall the deep and lasting impression that Brian made on him: "He was a great musician," Bachir remembered. "The greatest musician in the world I can say. Some day somebody will come to bring out this music of Jajouka to the world and to carve the memories of Brian Jones. Somebody will come. I have a feeling for that." Perhaps Bachir is intimating that the reincarnated Brian Jones may return to their isolated village, and so redeem a music which he was the first European to record.

Between the years 1967–69 Brian was almost permanently in a state of breakdown. With nobody to guide him out of this labyrinth, and with desperation on his part having him experiment with every form of substance which could bring some form of temporary relief to his suffering, Brian appeared to those in his immediate circle to be nothing more than a nervous wreck. The real events in Brian's life happened on an inner plane, and there's every reason to believe that he viewed the external world with such terror that whether or not he had been dismissed from the Rolling Stones it is doubtful that he would ever have toured again. He was of his own admission unable to cope with the rigorous physical demands of touring. What had attracted Brian to pop music was in part the need to prove himself a success in the face of an upbringing and education which had judged him a failure. Brian's revenge on his family was as extreme as anyone could achieve in twenty-six years. From the disparaged status of being essentially unemployed at the beginning of the 1960s, he rose within a few years to the dizzy apogee of being world famous as a musician in a band worshipped for its notoriety by a new monied generation. And in so doing Brian had succeeded in raising a demon which would almost immediately set about destroying him. While inwardly Brian relished fame and its accompanying privileges, outwardly he was ill-suited to meet the demands of a public who were as inherently hostile as they were irrationally adoring. Brian lived long enough to learn that success is conditional, and that for every admirer there is a corresponding detractor. There was a very real terror attached to being a successful sixties pop musician. With a crowd hysteria which was without precedent in the performing arena, and with a security which was often resentful of offering support to the act, Brian was to find his physical boundaries invaded by the uncontrollable mass. Whatever the power he assumed through daemonic forces, he was impotent to defend himself against the threat of physical attack. Brian faced the paradoxical situation of representing power as illusion. Few of his fans even in the crisis years, and largely because the Rolling Stones had stopped performing live at this period, could have anticipated the appalling state of Brian's nervous health. Apart from a brief appearance playing live at the *New Musical Express* poll winners concert at the Empire Pool, Wembley, in 1967, Brian remained – other than through the sensational medium of the media – concealed from his public. He had every reason at the time to be thankful for lack of direct public exposure.

If, as it has been suggested, Brian was epileptic, then he was obviously at pains to conceal the condition from himself and others. The problem would account for him blacking out on occasions, and undergoing mild fits. Terry Rawlings quotes George Chikiantz on the painful spectacle of witnessing Brian drop to the hotel floor in Tangier. What Chikiantz relates of the event appears as still another example of the callousness with which Brian was treated by his friends. According to Chikiantz: "Brian fell over – he suddenly went completely paralysed and fell over like a statue. Fortunately, he didn't go over the balcony. He just hit his head. I was quite alarmed, but Suki said: 'Brian does this every night. Just throw a blanket over him and leave him there.'"

Was it Brian himself who refused to seek medical help for his serious condition? Apart from his inveterately chronic asthma, and the distress it caused him, he seems only to have complained of acute or clinical depression. Are we to believe that nobody but Brion Gysin ever brought a doctor to Brian's assistance at the time of one of his attacks? Suki Potier's apparent negligence, and what amounts to her disregard for the fact that Brian habitually collapsed in this way – "Brian does this every night" – sounds like the brutal disinterest of one out-of-it person for another. Again and again in reviewing Brian's life we are made painfully aware that love, a great deal of sympathetic understanding and a genuine concern with the problematic aspects of his psychological behaviour, would if it had arisen in the right individual have saved him. The reverse side of this speculation is that Brian so completely identified with the role of sacrificial god that it was predestined that he should die young and at the hands of a generation he had indirectly attempted to redeem.

Recalling Brian's harassed and threatened predicament at the time of his worst excesses, Keith Richards has said this of the exacting pressures brought to bear on the terrified musician: "When the cops started leaning on Brian," Richards reflects, "the ones who ruled his area of London, they were vicious. They used to come for him regularly. Everything else he could have handled but with that kind of persecution on top, he was prone to a persecution complex anyway. But when it became a reality to him, Her Majesty's law coming through the door every day, he was so paranoid there wouldn't even be a bottle of booze around. The cops would walk in and immediately find some hash. He knew he didn't stand a chance."

Brian's life can be read as a reportage of assembled facts freeze-framed into a historic context, or those facts can be disassembled as we go in search of the real Brian, the one who reflected on his ruined life as he stared out of a police car window, or the one who must have thought long of a death which was always imminent. He lived in the fastest happening and most transitional decade of the twentieth century, but it's doubtful that he realised the importance of the events taking place around him. He was so much a part of them that there was little time for evaluation of their meaning in a social context.

Brian's psyche was like an underworld pool. The archetypes lived in its cloudy steam, and they comprised light and dark, the constructive and the daemonic. Given that all his boundaries were permeable, he was constantly troubled by the threatening nature of vision. He was invaded by autonomous phenomena which left him partly fascinated, but more often than not devastated. He was attracted to demons which also repelled him. Nobody around him was in touch with this level of experience and so he constantly felt isolated and persecuted. There was no mediating the hallucinatory properties of the free-floating images, and he discovered for himself that if he took drugs he increased the amplitude of what is called psychotic phenomena. The reason Brian felt drained of creative energies was because his hyperactive inner world asserted a compulsion far stronger than his needs to create as a musician. Brian wanted to enter so deeply into his interior that he needed to die in order to bring about a union with arcane knowledge. Like Narcissus, he couldn't part with his secret and so he drowned.

Brian's former girlfriend, Linda Lawrence, has recalled how he would sit up late in the kitchen writing poetic lyrics for potential songs. Sadly, none of Brian's writings seem to have escaped the unauthorised destruction or dispersal of his personal assets after his death at Cotchford Farm. The only surviving Brian Jones lyric appears to be "Thank You For Being There", the written text of which he deposited with the New York journalist Al Aronowitz. The lyric is, as one would expect, excavated from Brian's interior, and expresses the difficulties he had in distinguishing between imagination and reality. But the message of the song is a positive one, and the healing powers of love are given affirmative register over the terrors conjured out of Brian's unconscious by his high anxiety state. The second stanza of the lyric reads:

> *As I speak with you of love*
> *– In metaphors and in code*
> *A need for satisfaction grows*
> *But they're stories still to be told*
> *Of experience and fantasies*
> *Of vision and of fears*

But when the visions fade
– you'll be there
Lying in my tears
Thank you for being there my love
Then I know that you're real

The redemptive note sounded by the lyric is an important message from the real Brian – the person in dialogue with his inner world. The product of his anxiety, which he rightly alludes to as taking the form of threatening visions, is also redeemable through love. Whether the love is real or imagined, the ideal remains his comforter. The theme of Brian's lyric has something in common with the Gothic Romanticism of Edgar Allan Poe. Remembering that Brian lived in a paranoiac world, terrified of inner and outer realities alike, finding support in someone or something was vital to his sense of survival. Brian seems to have lived outside the context of assumed continuity in time which is the basis of ordinary day to day living. He observed no distinction between night and day – he got up when he would – and his approach to life was discontinuous in terms of structuring a future. His writing would have been an attempt to provide the psychic foundations which he lacked, looking inwards in order to facilitate the task of helping himself deal with the real world. This is exactly what Brian attempted to communicate in his poetic lyric.

If the lashing tail of paranoiac fears
Strike my smarting face
Your understanding comforts me
And puts everything in its place
So shush, my love,
Your look and your touch
can leave everything unsaid
And I can face all those
little people
Just like Gulliver did.
Thank you for being there, my love
At last I've found someone who's real

Given that the sixties as a decade defined the imaginatively poetic pop lyric, something that successive generations of lyricists have in large fallen short of, Brian's attempts to hold his own in a talented field are commendable. The powerful image resonant with his own anguished experience: "If the lashing tail of paranoiac fears/Strike my smarting face" is a moment of absolute self-realisation on Brian's part. Brian was continuously thought of as a paranoid by those who came to know him, but here is an instance of him discovering the truth for himself. He was never in denial of his disturbed mental state, but it's illuminating sometimes to turn the mirror round and have Brian speak for himself about the abyss which threatened his sanity. For the past thirty years we have been familiar with a Brian recreated by those who knew him, but the possible connotations of his one extant lyric serve to draw attention to how he perceived himself on the deepest level. Love, Brian tells us, will provide him with the strength to encounter his demons or "little people".

It's once again within the context of Gothic Romance, and with heavy undertones of Poe in the writing, that Brian concludes the final stanza of his song lyric.

> *The maniacal choirs that screamed out a warning*
> *Now sing our lullaby*
> *The walls that crashed to bury you and me*
> *Now shelter our hideaway*
> *Thank you for being there my love*
> *At last I've found someone that's real*
> *Thank you for being there my love*
> *At last I know that you're real*

In Brian's longing for emotional security he conceives of love as providing a house of shelter against the otherwise intrusive "maniacal choirs". All of Brian's deep-rooted persecution complex finds voice in this stanza. Brian must have been subject at times to "maniacal choirs" screaming out schizophrenic warnings in his head. His tendency to audio-hallucinate when he was undergoing a bad acid trip wasn't simply symptomatic of the drug, it was more a pointer to Brian's continually distressed mental condition. And while Brian secretly longed for a trusting and secure relationship, he would have rejected it outright if the possibility had arisen of his finding a sympathetic partner. If Brian ever really felt love for anyone, it was probably for Anita Pallenberg, and after the end of their destructive relationship friends spoke of Brian's inability to regain trust or even a modicum of self-esteem. For Brian, Pallenberg represented the symbol of 1960s liberation: she was attractive, independent, educated, and somehow seemed the logical extension of his own extravagantly feted public image. When Brian lost Anita to Keith Richards, his belief in music and the extraordinary decade in which he lived suffered a corresponding blow. Pallenberg's desertion left Brian disinherited of his sixties throne. Brian, far more than Mick Jagger, John Lennon or the flamboyantly charismatic Jimi Hendrix, had represented to his generation the dynamic which comes of uniting looks and creativity. Because the 1960s were as much about the expression of fashionable clothes as they were the adulation of pop musicians, so Brian had achieved a dominant place in the pantheon of the new icons who had successfully made a marriage between visual appeal and music. When Brian was faced with Pallenberg's desertion he not only suffered a profound private loss, but felt additionally humiliated in that news of his betrayal became public gossip. Brian understandably felt crest-fallen. In his mind the betrayal was still further consolidating evidence that he had not only been deposed as leader of his band, but that he had lost his status of acting as pop prince to his generation. Thereafter in clubs and boutiques along the King's Road, Brian felt that people were speaking pejoratively of him. The fact that Brian could have had any number of blonde clones by way of a substitute for Anita wasn't of course the issue. Brian had been seen to lose privately and publicly, and given his extreme sensitivity the double blow only served to accelerate his unfaltering commitment to a course of self-destruction. Brian was not only in this period of his life being told that as a musician he no longer fitted into the Rolling Stones, but he had additionally to bear the realisation that he was also a loser in love. In someone less insecure in themselves these events would not have assumed such monumentally catastrophic proportions, but given Brian's propensity for feelings of inferiority and self-hatred, he was never fully to recover from the way in which he lost Anita Pallenberg to Keith Richards.

It is generally acknowledged that Brian's mournful slide guitar contributions to *Beggar's Banquet* took the form of an elegiac valediction to his life as a Rolling Stone. As with his earlier plaintive guitar genius on "Little Red Rooster", his slide playing on the song "No Expectations" is an instance of Brian expressing his feelings of inner desolation within the context of the music he loved best: rhythm and blues. Perfectly empathising with the moribund nature of the song, Brian's guitar work amounts to funereal hints of his own last rites. His admirer Robert Palmer was to write much later in *Rolling Stone*, of how Brian's guitar part: "Did not sound remotely like that of any other musician – black, white, living or dead... In black folk culture," Palmer informs us, "slide playing has always spoken volumes. He must have outdone himself on 'No Expectations' because the song's story was his story, the feelings his feelings, as he could never have expressed them himself." "No Expectations" has Brian make the song his own in the way that Billie Holiday's subjective rendition of "Gloomy Sunday", otherwise known as "The Hungarian Suicide Song", appears to fit directly with the singer's desperate lifestyle. Brian's role as a musician was that of a gifted interpreter of other people's songs, a dignified mode of artistic expression which only became a disparaged act after sixties bands discovered it was far more lucrative to write their own material. Brian was in this sense an old-fashioned musician whose love was the creation of music itself, and whose personal achievement was in the skilled execution of the work. That he undoubtedly composed songs, but considered them too inferior to submit to the other members of the band, tells us as much about his reverence for good music, as it does about his psychological fear of rejection. And rather than face the possibilities of having work rejected Brian withdrew into an uncontactable private space fed by paranoid delusions. Even the compositionally uninspired Bill Wyman was to have a song accepted by the other members of the band for the album *Their Satanic Majesties Request*.

Although there was media noise that Brian was to be replaced by Eric Clapton as the new Rolling Stones guitarist, he was to attend the launch party for the release of *Beggar's Banquet* on 5 December 1968 at the Elizabethan Room of the Gore Hotel in London's Queensgate. The album had been extensively delayed due to the band's dispute with Decca over the artwork for the cover. Sensing still another storm of unwanted controversy surrounding the by now infamous Rolling Stones, Decca turned down the original artwork which depicted a graffiti-scrawled urinal, and the band unable to reach a compromise settled for a plain white RSVP sleeve. The candlelit reception to which guests were invited was later to devolve into a custard-pie battle, and Brian looking resplendent in lace and a grey silk top hat was to seek revenge on Jagger with a full pie-in-the-face volley.

On 21 November 1968, Brian had purchased Cotchford Farm, the former house of A.A. Milne, for the grand sum of £30,000, the purchase being conditional to the farm's housekeeper, Mrs Mary Hallett, staying on in Brian's employ. With his nerves worn down by police hassle, and in need of a refuge from the demands of a capital which Brian had come to associate with the scenes of his two arrests, Brian right from the start conceived of Cotchford Farm as a place in which he would set about restoring his damaged nerves. The rural retreat would also give him the necessary distance in which to reflect on the terrifying prospects of a future without the Rolling Stones. Events in this respect had continued to worsen, and Brian had reached a glacial point of non-communication with his estranged colleagues. It was a silence broken only by his joining them in mid-December at Wembley Studios for the filming of *The Rolling Stones's Rock and Roll Circus*, a project originally intended to be a TV spectacular for world distribution. Having hired a Big Top from Sir Robert Fassett's circus, complete with performing artistes, the band invited a list of acclaimed guests – including The Who, Eric Clapton, John Lennon and Jethro Tull – to participate in a rock extravaganza. The Rolling Stones were to premier a number of new songs and Brian, in what was to be his last ever appearance with the band he had so optimistically founded, was to contribute guitar to a repertoire which included "You Can't Always Get What You Want", "No Expectations", and "Parachute Woman". The recently released video of the Stones's performance shows a distinctly disorientated Brian playing memorable guitar flourishes, despite his evidently atrophied nerves. At the time Jagger considered the band's performance to be below standard, and this novel footage of Brian's last appearance with the Rolling Stones was to remain on hold for almost thirty years.

Brian meanwhile knew that as a consequence of his drug busts he had become a potential liability to the band in terms of future touring, and would in all probability be denied visa entry to Japan and the United States. Although the situation between him and the other members of the Rolling Stones was to remain broodingly dormant, it would sooner or later have to be articulated, and even if Brian was to keep his place in the band, a substitute would have to be considered for touring. On earlier occasions when Brian had been too unwell to perform, Keith Richards had maintained the band's guitar force by doubling for Brian, but the task was an unenviable one and unsatisfactory on a long term basis.

One of Brian's ways of dealing with the unresolved and unhappy situation was to disappear from contact with the group, and to spend progressively longer periods of time at his Cotchford retreat, returning to London on forays to make a round of his favourite clubs. Brian's newly acquired refuge – Cotchford Farm, situated fifty miles south-east of London, at Hartfield, Sussex – was a capacious property boasting six bedrooms, three reception rooms, garages, a staff apartment, and a heated swimming pool. Rather prophetically, Brian was to announce to a journalist at the time that he was so much in love with his rural acquisition, that he intended never to leave it: "I don't really know how to say it exactly," he pondered, "but there is magic about. A definite feeling. A force. It's something to do with what Milne created here I'm sure, but even more to do with me and my life. I feel as though I've always been here and always will be. I'll never leave here I'm sure." When Brian first arrived at Cotchford to take up residence there, he surprised the locals by his sartorial eccentricity. Combining a brown fur cape with purple and black stripe trousers, and with his dissolute features framed by a maroon-coloured Ascot hat, the villagers looked with suspicion on the farm's decadent new owner. But Brian, who was immediately attuned to the somnolent pace of rural life was, over the coming months, to find some sort of acceptance by the local community, most of whom regarded him as a threat only in terms of the noise generated by parties held at the house.

Brian intended Cotchford Farm to be his house of the imagination, and he filled it with his collection of priceless antiques, largely purchased over the years from his friend Christopher Gibbs's Chelsea antique shop. Prominent too were the woven rugs and furnishings which Brian had procured on his various sojourns in Morocco. He deliberated, as is the way with aesthetes, for a long time over finding the exact colour blue paint, for interior use, to remind him of the blue he associated with skies over Tangier. And on a similar level of colour associations Brian liked to sit and reflect by the swimming pool for the blue and green reflected water-lights reminded him, so he said, of Sweden.

As Brian settled into the fifteenth century farmhouse, and delighted in the privacy provided by a secret lane which came as part of the property, so the Rolling Stones were industriously recording their new single "Honky Tonk Women" at Olympic Studios, without his being invited to the sessions. It seemed that the band had unreservedly decided that Brian was too much of a health casualty to be of use to them as a recording and touring unit. In this intensely sad period for Brian, marking his still unannounced departure from the Rolling Stones, he would have his chauffeur drive him up to Olympic Studios, so he could listen outside to the sounds being created by a group of which he was still officially a member.

Parting with Brian wasn't an easy decision for the Rolling Stones. He was indubitably a visual asset to any band, and his talents as a gifted musical colourist were irreplaceable in the pop genre. If the Rolling Stones were to lose Brian, then their distinctly recognisable sound would change forever, a predicament of which they were only too well aware. There was also the distinct possibility that Brian would form his own group, and in doing so come to rival the Rolling Stones in terms of popularity.

On Brian's insistence that renovations be made to his newly acquired property, Keith Richards suggested that he hire a builder named Frank Thorogood, who had been responsible for the alterations carried out at Richards's Redlands property. Thorogood's dubious references went unchecked, his endorsement coming from his friend Tom Keylock, and at Thorogood's request three labourers with the names of Mo, Johnny and David were hired to assist with work at Cotchford Farm.

Frank Thorogood's estimate of £10,000 for the work in hand was outrageous in view of the relatively minor ameliorations to be made to the property. Brian, who was at the considerable disadvantage of being impractical in such matters, accepted the estimate unquestioningly, so establishing the precedent for Thorogood's progressively tyrannical manipulation of his affairs. Worse still for Brian was Thorogood's suggestion that he lived at Cotchford during the week, in order to facilitate the speedy expedition of work, and returned to his wife in London at the weekends. As an immediate sign of his duplicitous nature Thorogood moved into the garage flat with a girlfriend called Janet Lawson. And as a friend of Tom Keylock's, Thorogood was granted the power to draw money from the Stones's London office, which would then be charged to Brian's account. Unknown to Brian, Thorogood was also empowered by the Stones's organisation to be his minder, a role he carried out with a cruelty and despotism that had Brian come to feel a prisoner in his own home. In Brian's mind Thorogood, who was in his early forties, represented the viewpoint of an older generation whose beliefs he associated with his father's inflexible severity. There were very cogent reasons for Brian to instinctively dislike both Tom Keylock and Frank Thorogood, and Brian, who had already known friction with the militaristic Keylock, soon found the latter's counterpart in the cultureless Thorogood.

Brian initially had Suki Potier move in with him, and surrounded himself with an inherited family of cats and his two companionable dogs – a cocker spaniel called Emily and an Afghan hound which went by the name of Luther. He occupied himself with visits to Hartfield, and became an unobtrusive regular at the village pub The Hay Wagon, only his exotic clothes drawing attention to his essentially decadent manner.

Despite the obvious difference in his lifestyle from the local inhabitants, Brian took an active interest in their lives and seems to have succeeded in modifying his natural arrogance in their company. Brian always trusted simple people, and if he showed contempt to some of the minders at his disposal it was because he mistrusted their connivance with the nuclear power at work in the Rolling Stones's management.

Brian quickly converted what had been the property's lounge into a studio, and attentive to a busily fragrant log fire, he surrounded himself there with the eclectic panoply of costly instruments he had assembled over the years. He installed tape decks, a synthesiser, and recording facilities and set to work to give expression to a creative instinct which he considered had been repressed by his life as a pop musician. Brian's principal obsessions in music were still primarily jazz and blues, and whatever work in progress he committed to tape at this period would almost certainly have reflected these constants in his life.

However powerful the seductive spell asserted by Brian's insulated, bucolic world, his mental problems continued. Suki Potier grew terrified of Brian's emotional blanks, and saw herself as representing little more than habitual companionship to a man consumed by narcissism. Suki nurtured no illusions about Brian's inability to offer her love, and recalls: "Believe me, Brian was the only woman he ever really loved. Sometimes he would look right through me, staring off into space. I used to just make myself busy when he was like that as trying to get through to him was all but impossible." That Suki moved out of Cotchford Farm for good in March 1969 was a direct comment on how insufferable she found

Brian's self-indulgent behaviour. He was unapproachable to her on a level of intimate emotional sharing, and the vacuousness of being a woman living in the shadow of a pop star seemed to carry little appeal for her future.

What was apparent was that Brian was being cowed and bullied by the schemingly assertive Frank Thorogood. Thorogood took it on himself to charge his personal expenses to Brian's account, and despite the manifest incompetence of his work as a builder, he continued to increase his stranglehold over the frightened musician.

Brian was to reveal to Nicholas Fitzgerald on the afternoon of the day on which he died, that he had concealed about the house almost a hundred thousand dollars in cash, a sum which seems to have disappeared in the immediate events surrounding his death. Brian was not only murdered, but he was in addition robbed. Yet no enquiries were ever opened about the felonies committed at Cotchford Farm. The guests at Cotchford that night were spectators of Brian being held under in his swimming pool, according to Nicholas. They fled from the site in panic and were arguably those who looted the property. Or did that crime occur the following day, when Thorogood via Keylock again had access to the property? Somebody knew where Brian had stashed his money, and unlawfully grew rich on that knowledge. Brian had been used to paying his household staff in cash, and it was his habit to keep piles of banknotes by his bedside. Given the suspect characters of the builders employed at the house, it is more than probable that they took to stealing money in Brian's absence, and gutted the house after the murder had taken place. The innumerable unsolved questions surrounding the crimes committed against Brian on the night of 2 July 1969 have been masterfully examined by Geoffrey Giuliano and Terry Rawlings, both of whom include murder confessions in their respective biographies. But nobody has taken seriously the extensive nature of theft which took place that night and the day subsequent to the murder. With Nicholas Fitzgerald absent from the property at the time of events leading to Brian's death, Brian found himself without a single supportive friend in a house overtaken by drunken parasites. What part Anna Wohlin, who Brian had only known for a brief period of time, played in the cast of characters present that night is still unclear, but she was evidently powerless to control the situation. She was to leave the country almost immediately, with all manner of discrepancies in her statement remaining unquestioned by the local police. Was Anna threatened with death if she told the real story of what happened that night at Cotchford Farm? Brian was clearly in distress for a long time in the pool, as Thorogood and his accomplices repeatedly forced him under and refused him the right to leave the pool. None of this could have happened in complete silence. Are we to believe that Brian emitted no cry for help, and that the whole act took place like a scene in a silent movie? And anyhow, there's a psychic disturbance communicated in the air when somebody nearby is in a life-threatening situation. One neighbour reported hearing screams coming from Brian's property that night. The statements given at the time purport that Brian died mutely, and that the other inhabitants of the house came outside to discover his drowned body in the pool. The evidence reads as though Brian died a painless death with all the props carefully arranged like an unconvincing stage-set. But people don't disappear that easily. Neither I, nor the two investigative biographers who have established that Brian was murdered, believe that he died so conveniently.

Concerned about Brian's lack of communication with the other Rolling Stones, it was Mick Jagger who asked Brian's old friend Alexis Korner to visit him at Cotchford Farm, in the summer of 1969. It was Jagger's hope that Alexis would elicit from Brian the musical direction he intended to take with or without the Rolling Stones.

Korner, who had been originally responsible for giving Brian his first real break in music, was to remark on the physical changes which had overcome the ostracised Rolling Stone. To Korner Brian, in his extravagantly foppish clothes resembled "a fat mummified Louis the Fourteenth." Brian, who had renounced drugs under the paranoid threat of being re-arrested, was drinking heavily, and at one point fell asleep in mid-sentence. The regular consumption of brandy had caused Brian to unflatteringly put on weight, and the saturnine rings round his eyes accentuated his accelerating state of physical decline. But mentally, he was far from dispirited. Brian discussed with Korner the possibilities of his forming a new band, and even of his joining Korner's group The New Church for an upcoming German tour. Korner entertained the proposal before turning it down, foreseeing the potentially disastrous effects of touring with Brian in a state of chronic alcoholism. But importantly, Brian was alive to the idea of having a future independent of the Rolling Stones should they decide to dismiss him. Brian set about contacting names like Steve Marriot, who was in the process of forming the supergroup Humble Pie, John

Lennon, Jimi Hendrix's drummer Mitch Mitchell, John Mayall, Steve Winwood and the Vinegar Joe singer Elkie Brooks. He was reassured by the affirmative response he elicited from the cast of musicians he contacted; and with repeated visits from Alexis Korner Brian found the enthusiasm to start playing again. Korner was able to report to the Rolling Stones that he had got Brian playing his own material for long sessions, including one which had lasted 14 hours. There were signs that Brian's sloth-inducing depression was lifting, and Korner had sensitively succeeded in reactivating his old friend's confidence in his abilities to play. It would seem reasonable to assume that rehearsals would have been recorded, given that Brian had turned his music room into a rehearsal studio, and one can only assume that the relevant tapes were stolen or disposed of at the time of his death. The people on Brian's trail at Cotchford – and Brian repeatedly claimed to Korner that he was being held hostage there – seem not only to have deliberated his murder, but were adept at seeing that little or nothing of his personal possessions survived.

No matter how unnerving Brian may have found the suspense at Cotchford – he hourly anticipated the news arriving that he was no longer a member of the Rolling Stones – he retained his powerful belief in individual expression as central to the creative principle. "People used to say of me that I was too individualistic," Oscar Wilde wrote from prison; "I must be far more of an individualist than ever I was. I must get far more out of myself than ever I got, and ask for less of the world than ever I asked. Indeed, my ruin came not from too great individualism of life, but from too little."

Wilde's evaluation of himself as a man rejected by society on account of his individualistic bias, and therefore determined even in prison to increase those singular characteristics for which he had been punished, would have appealed to Brian in his unenviable situation. Brian waited and drank himself rotten.

It was on a sultry June evening that Mick Jagger, Keith Richards and Charlie Watts arrived at Cotchford Farm to confront Brian with the issue of his leaving the band, if not permanently, then at least for the foreseeable future. Brian himself expressed a disinclination to tour, stating that his health could no longer take it, and he was offered a down-payment of £100,000 on leaving the band, together with an assured £20,000 per annum for as long as the group existed.

If the deal in effect offered Brian some vestige of financial security, then it also deprived him of the special glamour attached to being a member of the world's foremost rock band. It wasn't without distinct feelings of personal loss that Brian accepted the terms of the settlement, and a press statement was released to the effect that Brian Jones had left the Rolling Stones on account of differences of musical opinions with Mick Jagger. Over the next few days Brian was to plummet through air-pockets of self-doubt as he pondered on the reality of what he had let go, and faced up to his uncertain future. He was determined to succeed in his new career, if for no other reason than to prove his superiority to a band who had dismissed him. And with the full services of the Rolling Stones's publicity office still available to him, Brian was understandably optimistic about the chances of his continuing as a successful pop musician.

Yet work at the farm was still far from complete, and Frank Thorogood and Tom Keylock continued to hold conspiratorial court in Brian's house. For the time being Brian found himself suspended in an oasis of uncertainty. His main payment from the Stones's New York office had still not materialised, his rehearsals with a new band in mind were still at a formative stage, and his property was policed by exploitative builders. The final stage in the plot was about to evolve.

FIVE: **NARCISSUS MURDERED**

"I – I who call myself magus or angel, exempt from all morality, am now returned to the earth, with a duty to pursue and a hard reality to embrace."

—Arthur Rimbaud

Brian's brief summer in 1969 was drawing to a rapid conclusion. With Anna Wohlin ensconced in the house, and with the unwelcome and parasitic presence of Frank Thorogood and his three hired building labourers, Brian was to complain of lights being shone into the farm at night, and of his being intimidated by a vindictive Thorogood. Even more sinister – spotlights were in the process of being put up around the pool, as though an execution site was being prepared for the still uncomprehending victim.

The premises of Brian's psychological life during his years as a famous musician were largely hero-based. To Thorogood and his scheming retinue Brian represented a narcissistic poseur, a wealthy and self-appointed elitist, and more importantly an unassertive fallen hero. That Brian was at times out of control either due to illness or heavy drinking, made it seem as though he could be easily manipulated. Brian appeared to the dishonest Thorogood to have inexhaustible wealth at his disposal. He kept cash-stashes in the house, was visited by attractive girls, regularly invited the London glitterati to Cotchford Farm, and seemed to be an easy target to be divested of his remaining fortune. What developed at Cotchford that summer was that a crude male camaraderie existing between Thorogood and his three associates became excited first by the prospects of robbing Brian, and second by the perverse thrill of killing him. Brian's death must in part be attributed to homophobia. So called "straight" bravado fuelled by a desire to prove its masculinity will, if encouraged by a group-spirit, turn on a man who manifests feminine characteristics. This ugly trait which substitutes a male victim for the perpetrators' lack of prowess with women has its roots in gender confusion. Homophobes may be insecure about their own latent sexual attraction to men, and so attempt to compensate for these feelings by aggressive behaviour towards gay men. But there's an interesting characteristic here which applies to Brian's particular case. Homophobes invariably associate effeminacy with homo-sexuality. They are unlikely to pick on a fitness clone. The butch or masculine gay is left alone by their group. The homophobic victim, whether of verbal abuse or assault, is invariably somebody like Brian, a person resented by the tenets of machismo for having deserted traditional male values.

A.E. Hotchner, the author of *Blown Away*, an investigative book on the Rolling Stones, interviewed a participant in or a direct eye-witness to the homophobic events surrounding Brian's murder. This person, disguised in the book under the name of Marty, professed that: "There was two guys in particular had it in for Brian, I mean, always making remarks, 'the rich fag', all that kinda stuff. They used to pinch stuff off Brian all the time. Anyway, this night Brian was swimming a lot. He could swim good, bounce off the diving-board, lots better than any of us lads and the girls was watching him, also because he was a celebrity they sort of gave him attention. These two guys got pissed about that – they was drinking pretty good by then – it was kind of like, when it started, like teasing. Sort of grabbing Brian by the leg and pulling him down, meanwhile saying bitchy things, just horsing around, but kind of rough. Sort of interfering with his swimming.   "...Brian tried to get out of the pool and they wouldn't let him, kept pushing him back and pulling him under and then it started to get rough and these lads really got worked up at Brian the more he resisted... I guess they were just wanting to throw a scare into him, I don't know... I could tell it was turning ugly as hell.

"One lad wanted to get Brian out, but the other wouldn't let him and they was kind of tugging on him. It got real crazy and then the next thing I heard was somebody say, 'He's drowned...' Got to our cars in one hell of a hurry and cleared out."

From the evidence supplied by "Marty" we have to assume that Frank Thorogood was one of the two murderers, or that he supplied the finishing touches when Brian was already partially drowned. Was that what Thorogood meant when he confessed to Tom Keylock on 7 November 1993, the day before he died: "It was me that did Brian... I just finally snapped, it just happened. That's all there is to it." In his 1969 statement given to the police Thorogood had claimed that he and Brian had been alone together swimming in the pool, and that after he had briefly left the water to find a cigarette in the house, he had returned minutes later to find Brian dead at the bottom of the pool. A likely re-staging of events could have it that Brian was left for dead in the pool after having been repeatedly held under by two of Thorogood's acquaintances, and that Thorogood took Brian's life as the hysterical guests disappeared. Thorogood may have been in the house at the time drinking, and this would explain the notion of him going outside to find Brian in the pool. Only that he went to the pool not with the aim of rescuing Brian, but with the intention of killing him.

Marty's evidence accords perfectly with Nicholas Fitzgerald's account of what happened at Cotchford Farm that night. Nicholas Fitzgerald and his friend Richard Cadbury had been waiting at Haywards Heath station for a friend of Brian's to materialise, and did not return to Cotchford until around 11.00 p.m. When their car pulled into Cotchford Lane they were confronted by the headlights of a driverless car, the engine still running, parked in the middle of the road. Aware that something wasn't quite right – there was a silence pervading the farm instead of the sound of amplified music – Fitzgerald and his friend decided to approach the house from the back, gaining admission through a hole in the hedge leading into Bluebell Wood. Coming within sight of the house and pool, Nicholas could make out activities going on under the pool spotlights. Nicholas has described his findings meticulously: "At the far right-hand corner of the swimming pool three men were standing... The power of the spotlights blotted out their features... The middle one dropped to his knees, reached into the water and pushed down on the top of a head that looked white.

"At the opposite corner of the pool – far left – stood two other people, a man and a woman, gazing down into the pool where the kneeling man said something. It sounded like a command and I caught the words, '...do something'. At that, the third man on that side jumped into the water the way an animal might jump, arms out-stretched, knees bent. He landed on the back of the struggling swimmer. The man who snapped out the command seemed to be preparing himself also to jump in...

"Suddenly, out of the bushes next to me, stepped a burly man wearing glasses. He grabbed my shoulder... 'Get the hell out of here, Fitzgerald, or you'll be the next.' It was a cockney accent. I was terrified. He meant it."

Who were the man and woman coolly observing Brian in the process of being brutalised by these three individuals? They were obviously complicitous in what was going on for they made no attempt to come to Brian's assistance. We infer from this that they were in on Thorogood's activities. The police statement named only two women as having been present at the house that night. Janet Lawson, who was in fact Thorogood's mistress, and Anna Wohlin who had moved in with Brian several weeks earlier. We know nothing of relations between these two women, and of how if at all they interacted on a daily basis. Certainly Frank Thorogood's inveterately contemptuous attitude to Brian must have been communicated to Janet over their months of shared living at Cotchford Farm. Wouldn't it have seemed logical for the enquiry into Brian's murder to have explored the ugly relations which had existed between Frank Thorogood and Brian for the entire period in which building work had been carried out at Cotchford Farm? As it was, three radically contradictory statements given by the key witnesses to Brian's body being discovered drowned in the pool were accepted as evidence that he had died as a result of misadventure. Brian's death certificate was to attribute the cause of his drowning to: "severe liver dysfunction due to fatty degeneration and the ingestion of alcohol and drugs. Swimming whilst under the influence of alcohol and drugs. MISADVENTURE". Despite the fact that the autoptical findings were to refute the information supplied by Brian's death certificate, the matter was again considered closed.

It was Geoffrey Giuliano who, while researching his book *Paint It Black*, was contacted by one of the accomplices to Brian's murder. In need of confessing the crime to which he was a party, the character pseudonymously named Joe provided an account of the murder similar to that given by Marty in *Blown Away*. I quote from Joe's acrimonious confession: "I put me hands on his shoulders, pushed him under and pulled him up by the hair. It went on for a quarter of an hour or so. The last time he just fucking went down. He didn't fight, didn't do anything. It was Frank that kept pushing him... Frank had got him by the shoulders and we was pushing him and he weren't fighting back. He weren't doing nothing. So we thought, 'fucking hell,' and we let him go and he didn't do nothing. Frank says, 'He's fucking dead!' I says, 'Let's get the fuck out of here for fuck's sake!' Now Frank, he's got this old Ford Anglia and he says, 'Quick, get out, get fucking dressed. No don't even bother getting dressed, just grab your clothes. You can do it in the car. I'll get the clothes. Let's get the fuck out of here.' We jumped out of the pool and we left him there. He weren't at the bottom, but he weren't at the top. He was sort of halfway."

The Frank referred to in Joe's confession was a casual labourer on the property. Joe refused to give the names of the other accomplices to the crime, and claimed to have changed his appearance from a hippy to a skinhead, and to have pursued a fugitive life in London subsequent to the murder. According to Joe, "we expected they were going to be scouring the country for these hippies that killed Brian Jones. You know, we thought, 'big murder, big pop star'. I mean, it weren't like killing the bloke round the corner, was it? It's 'Brian Jones', you know. But nothing happened."

If we are to believe the accounts provided respectively by Marty and Joe of Brian's being killed by a number of hands, then once again the time factor is of importance here. Brian, as it seems probable, was drowned over a period of fifteen minutes. This a is a long time in which to be in distress, and something of his crisis would have been communicated to all who were at Cotchford Farm that night. According to Brian's housekeeper, Mrs. Hallett, she was alerted by the sound of "terrified screaming. My daughter said she heard screaming and I got up and went down to the bottom of the path. I was only in my night-dress so I turned around and came back in quick."

It would seem to me that everyone at the house that night knew precisely what was happening to Brian. A collective homophobic spirit spiralled out of control, and the spectators to rough play found themselves secretly participating in the chain of aggressive energies. One can see it almost as possession. People were afraid to intervene on Brian's behalf, and perhaps found themselves wilfully acceding to events. Was Anna Wohlin the source of the screaming described by Mrs. Hallett as issuing from a woman's voice? In the sequence of events described in *Paint It Black* by Joe, it could equally have been one of the casual labourers' girlfriends who panicked on realising that Brian was dead. This is a notion purely tangential to the findings raised by Giuliano in *Paint It Black*.

Parties were commonplace events in the sixties. They were an expression of a newly-won youth culture, and party activities such as doing soft drugs or imbibing quantities of alcohol centred round the dynamic of playing pop music. It was the music which served as a stimulus to sensory activities. From what we learn there was a party almost every night at Brian's house. These were informal occasions encouraged by the presence of a group of young men who were working on the property. On the night that Brian died, an unspecified number of people, probably 10–12, formed the basis of the impromptu party at Cotchford Farm.

Nicholas Fitzgerald had arrived at Cotchford early in the afternoon of 2 July 1969, and Brian had come to meet him at the Hay Wagon pub. Nicholas had tried repeatedly to reach Brian by telephone the night before, and always unsuccessfully. He was met by a Brian who looked excessively paranoid. According to Nicholas's account: "It was seeping into my mind that Brian really was in some kind of danger. He looked terrible now, though stone-cold sober. He was haggard and drawn, and his eyes were like a hunted animal's." Brian quickly made it known to Nicholas that he was being massively exploited by the builders at his house, and that he was almost a captive in his own property. "We'd better go back," Brian told Nicholas, "but I want to talk some more at the house. Please stay with me tonight, Nicholas. Just to hold me."

Fitzgerald's account leaves little doubt that the restively intimidated Brian had been threatened with reprisals if he spoke about the improprieties conducted at Cotchford Farm. With Brian no longer a member of the Rolling Stones, even though their office was financing repairs at the house, he was in a transitionally vulnerable phase of his career. To the unscrupulous it was the perfect time to take advantage of his weaknesses. What sort of hold was it that Frank Thorogood and his associates had on Brian? We know that they physically intimidated the easily frightened musician, but the level of their criminality possessed deeper roots. Had Brian been set up sexually, and blackmailed? Were this party of dubious characters being paid to see that Brian didn't establish the all-star group with John Lennon and Jimi Hendrix of which he had spoken? Geoffrey

Giuliano's taped interview with Joe led to the tangential issue of money, or more exactly a pay-off. Joe admitted to having been given £350 by his accomplice Frank on the grounds that he maintained silence, while Frank's lifestyle went upmarket, as though he had acquired handsome remuneration for his completed act.

Back to Nicholas Fitzgerald's account of Brian's last afternoon. Nicholas, sitting outside with Brian in the vicinity of the pool, observed: "Brian looked up as two men came walking past. They were perhaps in their thirties, scruffily dressed and with longish hair. One was carrying a guitar case. They passed within a few yards of us without speaking to us or even acknowledging our existence." As if this calculatedly nonchalant disrespect for Brian were not sufficient an indication of his loss of territorial control, Brian became agitated by the fact that two spotlights had been that day installed at the pool. Nicholas reports Brian as commenting: "I don't know why the servants think it's so important to have two spotlights. They've been tinkering around here all day with them. What do they want two spotlights for?" Brian was to go on to say: "Nicholas, I'm bloody scared. Scared out of my mind that they'll try to stop me... They know I'm in a position to start this new band. They know it could knock the Stones out of the charts. It's my name and the fans will know it's me. It'll be bigger than the Stones. I've done it once and I can do it again."

It was then that Brian complained to Nicholas of having seen lights flashing on and off in the trees at night, and of having heard a car circling the lanes. It would be easy to attribute such phenomena to Brian's paranoid disposition, but somehow his reported fears as they were told to Nicholas ring true. The fact that he had asked Nicholas to sleep with him that night suggests that Brian's relationship with Anna Wohlin wasn't predominantly sexual. It was to Nicholas to whom Brian was turning for comfort and reassurance. In addition to Brian's anxiety about some of the dubious people employed on his property, he had for a long time lived with the fear that there was a contract out on his life. Fitzgerald tells us: "When I had first come to know Brian in 1965 he wouldn't go out of doors until after dark because he believed someone was out to harm him – someone in the US and someone in London. He told me Bob Dylan had warned him that there was a contract out on his life."

If we ask ourselves why was somebody out to get Brian, then inevitably we return to the Wildean notion of individualism. Brian was individual in ways that both shocked and disquieted his contemporaries. He also paid for illegal drugs with cash, and so must have had an insider's knowledge of the dealers who supplied the pop world and their entourage. Like Wilde, Brian's culture had been open to corruption, and his life as a famous musician had taken him by detours into the underworld. Was Brian's death in part instigated and financed by nefarious drug barons? The beginning of Wilde's end was that he had trusted the hired rent boys with whom he had consorted. Being generous himself he had not anticipated the duplicity in others. There is no record of Wilde having exploited or morally corrupted any of the youths who were paid to give evidence against him. He treated them by their code exemplarily: he paid them honestly for their sexual favours. But with Brian, did he simply know too much about the ethos of dealers, who in turn feared that if the police interrogated him again, he would speak? It should be remembered that Brian had been run out of town by police harassment, and was likely thereafter always to be kept under scrutiny.

There were other murky eddies in Brian's undertow, like the various illegitimate children he had irresponsibly disowned, and the women whom he had neglected in the process. Whether consciously or unconsciously Brian had been responsible for breaking lives. He had cared nothing for the outcome of his actions. A great deal of the poignancy surrounding Brian's last hours is brought out by the sensitive vignette that Nicholas Fitzgerald has left of his last meeting with his friend. Nicholas, who is adamant that Brian played him a rehearsal tape on which John Lennon and Jimi Hendrix were part of the musical cast, remembers: "This picture of him is the one which, because of what happened later, will always remain in my mind: a helpless boy who had scarcely reached maturity and yet had experienced phenomenal success as well as unendurable despair. As I looked at him with his head tilted back as if in final defiance of a world that had showered him with wealth and yet left him so alone, I felt tears coming to my eyes, quickened by the pathos of the music."

Nicholas was called away from the house by Brian requesting that he drive to Haywards Heath station to collect a female friend named Luciana Martinez Delarosa, who was due down from London that evening. By the time he and his friend were to return to Cotchford farm several hours later Nicholas was to witness Brian's death at the hands of three men. He was to narrowly avoid being murdered himself.

In spite of the detailed confessions of two men who claimed to have been directly instrumental to Brian's death, and to Frank Thorogood having admitted to Tom Keylock on his deathbed that he "did Brian", there are still those who maintain that Brian died of natural causes. But according to forensic medicine, there is no evidence of Brian having undergone cardiac arrest, still less of his having suffered and asthmatic attack, while swimming. For a regular drinker like Brian the quantity of alcohol found in his blood – 0.14, which is no more than the equivalent of 3½ pints of beer – would have been unlikely to have contributed to his death. The amphetamine compound found in his urine, and not affecting his blood barbiturate level, was from the prescribed drugs Durophet and Valium which Brian regularly took. Pathological findings suggest that Brian did not die as a consequence of intoxication. While findings revealed fatty degeneration of his liver, this condition was not the cause of Brian's death. Ingenious research by Geoffrey Giuliano has established through the forensic overview of Dr. Cyril H. Wecht that Brian could easily have been repeatedly dunked by the force of hands on his head without there being any trace of bruising on his body. Viewed in these terms, it was the perfect murder. Water erases fingerprints, and his assailants without forceful body contact could have drowned Brian by repeatedly having him swallow water. Paramount to the situation is that Brian was by all accounts an excellent swimmer. His agility in the water and his abilities to dive and swim for long periods totally discount the accepted opinion that he sank to the bottom of his pool in the brief period in which Frank Thorogood left him alone. Such an event given Brian's aquatic prowess was not only improbable, but in all likelihood impossible. The only way in which Brian would have disappeared in a time-span of five minutes was if the had suffered a heart attack. It takes time to drown an experienced swimmer, and Joe's confession that he and his friend Frank set about repeatedly holding Brian under for a period of fifteen minutes is probably accurate. Nicholas Fitzgerald describes the drowning as the work of three men. In his account of the murder, the man who finally jumped onto Brian's back, was needed for additional force. The proposition is certainly open to conjecture.

After his death Brian was treated by the authorities as a disposable fact. His death's-head was raised as a warning to the young that he exemplified a lifestyle which had resulted in an ignominious, early demise. A self-righteous establishment felt vindicated by the manner of his dying. As Brian's name had been publicly associated with drugs, the latter phenomenon was the most advantageous criterion on which to hang his death. At the time the idea of Brian having drowned due to excess of drugs and alcohol went almost unquestioned. To the press it appeared as though he had earned a justified nemesis for a life devoted to youthful hedonism. Nobody considered that Brian was in large a cultured, painfully introspective being whose nerves had been shattered by the public exposure attendant on fame. Instead, he was perceived by the media as a necessary scapegoat for a liberal ethos which had got out of control.

Recalling how Brian readily identified with the white goat sacrificed and eaten by the Jajoukans in Morocco, raises once more the powerful symbol of the scapegoat. He commented to friends at the time that it was himself who he was eating. Brian had witnessed his metaphoric death in the mountains as an initiatory precedent to the physical death he was to undergo by water. In the book of Leviticus in the Old Testament and according to Jewish rites of atonement, and after having performed the necessary ceremonies for the expiation of the holy place: "Aaron shall lay both his hands upon the head of the live goat and confess over him all the iniquities of the children of Israel, and all their transgressions even all their sins, and he shall put upon them the head of the goat and shall send him away by the hand of a man that is in readiness into the wilderness and the goat shall bear upon him all their iniquities unto a solitary land and he shall let the goat go in the wilderness."

Brian had lived for years in a psychic space identifiable as the wilderness. He had found himself exiled by his own band, made solitary by his lack of trust in a sycophantic entourage, and finally isolated in a country house overtaken by quasi-builders who were there for no other reason than to parasitically drain Brian of his remaining wealth. Brian's bank account at the time of his death stood at £4,000, and without the promised remuneration stemming from his pay-off by the Stones's management, he would soon have been in debt to his builders. Any record deal for his new band would have taken time to negotiate, and so Brian had reason to be troubled by the unreal demands placed on his finances by Frank Thorogood.

There are many variants of the psychological connotations implied by the scapegoat and the story of the god being chased into the underworld. In one of the myths derived from the Dionysiac cult, the goat dies as an expiatory sacrifice for having attacked the vine. In this instance the god dies for a sin committed by him. As the Dionysian symbol of the vine implies intoxication, or correspondingly the phallus, then implicit in this form of sacrificial death is the notion of a self-destructive offence. Brian went against the grain of his sensibility by constantly drinking too much. What began in his case as private drinking – he would keep his bottle concealed in an airline bag on tour – was to escalate into a landsliding alcoholism. In terms of Dionysian mystery Brian was guilty of having attacked the vine or his individual godhead.

But Dionysus, like Orpheus, was dismembered, a death we may read as a form of castration, and one that is mitigated into a second birth. It will be remembered that Orpheus was destroyed on account of his homosexuality, and that his severed head continued to sing even after it was thrown into the river. Orpheus was killed by women raving against his effeminacy. Brian was ritually sacrificed because of a difference in him which was construed by his base murderers as homosexuality. In most stories the expulsion of the scapegoat merges into the ritual of carrying out or destroying death. Brian had only weeks before his death been expelled from the Rolling Stones. He had as a result of this become effectively an outcast. Some sort of encounter with death was the inevitable outcome of Brian's expulsion from the tribe. This would account for the portentous sense of apprehension which invaded Brian for the weeks preceding his death.

We are told that when the Titans killed Dionysus they painted themselves white all over with gypsum. They adopted this disguise so that they would not be recognised as the murderers of the deity. Interestingly Dionysus's heart was rescued by Zeus, the father of the gods, and so his integral organ remained unmolested by his adversaries. Initiates into the mystery were painted white in memory of the Titans, a metaphor we may extend to the perception that Mick Jagger chose to wear a white Mr. Fish dress on the occasion of Brian's memorial concert in Hyde Park.

In terms of the mythological, death finds its interface in rebirth, and so the two psychological states are unified through continuity. In Brian's case, his death has given rise to a cult which persists to this day and is likely to go on doing so, for as long as Brian's music is remembered. One can rightly call Brian's fans initiates into a mystery cult. The young god has disappeared but his legacy continues through the constancy of his devotees.

Geoffrey Giuliano's research into Brian's death has succeeded in radically deconstructing the statements given by the three principle witnesses to finding Brian drowned in his pool. Giuliano has pointed out the glaring inconsistencies in the accounts given respectively by Frank Thorogood, Janet Lawson and Anna Wohlin. The sequence of events reported by the three witnesses should have alerted the police to discrepancies particularly in relation to conflicting times given for the sequence of events, and contradictory reports as to who found Brian and attempted to lift him from the bottom of the pool.

According to Frank Thorogood, a man whom Brian had every reason to dislike, Brian accepted his invitation for a late night swim, soon after watching *Rowan and Martin's Laugh-In* on television. Why we ask should Brian have agreed to share a recreational swim with a man who had been intimidating and defrauding him for a period of almost six months? Brian had expressed his extreme distaste for Frank Thorogood to close friends like Nicholas Fitzgerald. Thorogood's evidence relied on his continued assertion that Brian was inebriated before they entered the pool. According to Thorogood, Anna Wohlin was also initially in the pool, and if this was the case, then why wasn't Anna aware of Brian's unstable condition? Why did she risk leaving Brian alone with a man who was quite obviously capable of doing him harm? Why wasn't Anna watching out for him?

According to Thorogood the two women present at Cotchford Farm that night, Janet Lawson and Anna Wohlin, had both retreated indoors by the time he took a break from swimming with Brian, and went into the house. Thorogood's official statement claims: "After we had been in the pool for about twenty minutes or so, I got out and went to the house for a cigarette leaving Brian in the pool. I honestly don't remember asking Janet for a towel, but if she said I did, I accept it. I know I got a cigarette and lit it and when I went back to the pool, Anna appeared from the house about the same time. She said to me, 'He is lying on the bottom,' or something like that. I saw Brian face down in the deep end on the bottom of the pool. Anna and I got in the water and, after a struggle, got him out. His body was limp and as we got him to the side, Janet joined us and helped get him out."

Immediately flawed in Thorogood's statement is his attempt

to win favour by claiming fallibility over the minor point as to whether he was or wasn't handed a towel by Janet Lawson. And why should Anna have appeared from the house at the exact moment that Thorogood chose to return to the pool? And where, as Giuliano has questioned, were Brian's two faithful dogs in the sequence of events? Wouldn't they have sensed that Brian was in trouble and have come yelping out of doors? According to Thorogood's statement Anna appears to have expressed no emotion on finding Brian obviously drowned, but "said to me, 'He is lying on the bottom,' or something like that." In this account Anna's emotional register is made to sound nonchalantly casual, as though she is referring to a stranger.

Janet Lawson contradicts Frank's statement by claiming that she preceded Thorogood out to the pool, while Anna at the time was upstairs on the telephone. "I shouted under the open window of the bedroom to Anna who was speaking on the telephone. I ran into the house and shouted to Frank. Both joined me, I was by then in the water, but realised I couldn't manage him alone and I shouted to Frank to get into the pool to get Brian out. I returned to the house to use the phone, but I had difficulty as the line was engaged and there were several telephones in the house, but I was not sure of the locations of them all."

If as Janet claimed, both Anna And Frank joined in the effort to retrieve Brian from the bottom of the pool, then how was the house line still engaged? Who was using the telephone indoors, when the other two occupants of the house were attending to Brian at the pool? The contradictions inherent in the official statements discredit any notion of the truth. And why was it that Janet Lawson, as a trained nurse, should have taken it on herself to abandon Brian, and rush into the house? Shouldn't she have sent Anna or Frank running for the telephone, while she applied her practical skills to endeavouring to resuscitate Brian? Instead, Janet lost precious time in going back to the house before finally returning to give Brian cardiac massage. In Frank Thorogood's statement it was Anna who first sighted Brian on the bottom of the pool, and in Janet Lawson's statement she claims to have discovered Brian drowned at a time when Frank and Anna were both still in the house. Anna was on the telephone upstairs, and presumably Frank was still relaxing with his cigarette. The lack of any synchronicity in the official statements given to the police should have been sufficient in itself to have prompted a murder investigation, particularly in that a group of rough casual labourers had been working on the property for a number of months. It should have been obvious to the police that Frank Thorogood and his associates were not Brian's sort of people. Brian had in fact proposed firing Frank Thorogood that very evening, and the idea of murder constituting an act of revenge for dismissal cannot under the circumstances be ruled out.

Here again we are faced with an instance of the sad social misconceptions which coloured the sixties. Because Brian was a member of an infamous pop band, and because he dressed in a way that drew attention to himself, the general public were of the opinion that he represented lowlife. They were only too anxious to misjudge his character. The authorities knew nothing of this sensitive young man's education, refinement and general culture, nor of his considerable gifts as a musician. If these aspects of Brian had been taken into account by the police, then perhaps suspicion would have been provoked by a character like Frank Thorogood having a free run of Brian's property. Why were none of the builders at Cotchford Farm ever called into question?

Returning to Nicholas Fitzgerald's detailed account of the events leading to murder; frustrated by the non-arrival of Brian's friend at Haywards Heath station, Nicholas and his friend, Richard Cadbury, decided to telephone Brian to say that they had abandoned their wait and were returning to the farm. In Nicholas's words: "Using the telephone in the foyer I dialled the number. A girl's voice said, 'Hello?' I asked to speak to Brian. There was no answer. In the background I could hear a lot of noise and loud music, as if a party was going on. This struck me as odd. Brian hadn't mentioned any party and there had hardly been anyone about when we had left. Could Luciana have arrived with a bunch of friends? I said, 'Hello?' There was still no reply – only the sound of revelry. After no one had answered about three minutes later, someone put the phone down at the other end. What the hell was going on? I hadn't recognised the girl's voice on the telephone. It hadn't sounded foreign. Why had she refused to answer that first hello? Had someone taken the handset from her? Perhaps Thorogood, or one of the other employees – Keylock? I looked at my watch. It was five to ten."

What Nicholas had picked up on immediately was what would have been apparent to everyone at the house, and that is a sense that something was not quite right. Nicholas felt the beginnings of nervous apprehension, and finally persuaded Richard Cadbury to drive him back to Cotchford Farm, the two of them coming to within sight of the house by 11.15 p.m.

The cacophonic noise with which Nicholas had intersected on the telephone was clearly the drunken loutishness of a party which had rudely taken over the house. Although Brian's ordeal was probably not to begin until 11:00 – the participant Joe claimed that Brian was drowned over a period of approximately fifteen minutes – clearly things at the house had started to get ugly. I believe that Brian's murder was predetermined, and that a complicitously homophobic spirit conspired that night to take his life. Events were possibly building along those lines by the time Nicholas scented danger at 10:00.

Interestingly, why does Nicholas appear to take it for granted that Tom Keylock was at the house that night? According to Keylock he had been sent on a mission by Keith Richards who was recording at Olympic Studios, London, that night, to retrieve a guitar from Richards' Redlands property. We have had cause to remark that Brian disliked Tom Keylock every bit as much as he loathed his associate Frank Thorogood. Keylock was in effect Thorogood's employer, and was to supply the press with select information when they gathered outside Cotchford Farm on the morning of 3 July 1969, in the wake of Brian's death.

Still another question of identity, who was the powerfully built man, wearing glasses, who forced Nicholas off the property on his return, after hitting his friend Richard Cadbury in the face? This man spoke with a Cockney accent, and was an insider to Brian's private life, for he knew Nicholas by name. It seems certain that this man who was in Brian's confidence had learned from him that at some stage in the evening Nicholas and his friend would be returning to Cotchford Farm. Hadn't Brian asked Nicholas earlier in the day to spend the night with him? When Nicholas telephoned the house at 10:00, and was denied the right to speak to Brian, suspicion must have been out for his return. Now in a quiet rural district you can distinctly listen out for the approach of a car, in this case along Maresfield Road and into Cotchford Lane. Nicholas and Richard Cadbury were to be forced out of their car by a stationary vehicle parked as an obstruction in Cotchford Lane. There's every reason to believe that the offending vehicle, placed there with its headlights on, had been deliberately positioned as a decoy. While the murder was taking place in the pool, someone had been stationed to the rear of the property to anticipate Nicholas's return. He or they would have heard Cadbury's car enter into Cotchford Lane, and then stall at the sight of an immobile car. This move would not only have played for time, but it was calculated to force the two young men out of their car. Had they driven up to the house and witnessed events, then they could quickly have turned about and driven off to summon immediate help. As it was, they were delayed in their arrival, but not sufficiently to prevent them witnessing the murder. Now whoever was waiting for Nicholas knew perfectly well that there was a way into Bluebell Wood to the rear of the house by an unclosed gap in the hedge. To be possessed of this knowledge would have come from being conversant with the property's access-points, and who better than a team of builders who were permitted regular entry to the property. Somebody had chosen to cover the ingress to the house which was the only way open to Nicholas and his friend. Once inside, the two young men, betrayed by their crackling footsteps, managed to get as far as the summerhouse and to remain in the building's shadow. It was from this concealed vantage point that Nicholas was able to perceive Brian's death-throes, as he was repeatedly held under water. By the time a fist was presented to his face by a man emerging from the bushes, Nicholas had uncomprehendingly watched Brian's final assailant jump on to his back like an animal. Brian had obviously been attempting to fight back at this point, for the command, 'do something' which Nicholas heard snapped out in the night air was clearly an incisive order to kill. Nicholas was forcibly pushed back into Bluebell Wood, where he was preceded by Richard Cadbury who was bloodied by a head gash. There was no arguing point in this brutal contact, for Nicholas was identified and threatened should he attempt to resist his combatant.

From Nicholas's sightings it is clear that it took three men to despatch Brian. Frank and Joe as they are pseudonymously named in *Paint It Black* clearly had a problem in drowning a remarkably resilient swimmer, and evidence would suggest that a third man was called for to successfully keep the struggling swimmer down, before he died.

That there may have been others earlier on involved in scaring Brian seems equally possible. The collective homophobic pack had probably thinned, once the less committed of the assailants realised that things were getting out of hand. As the dynamic behind any mob is cowardice fuelled by aggression, so those intent on dissociating themselves from what was clearly going to result in Brian's death, scrambled out of the pool. Some of the pack probably feared reprisals from their girlfriends, for we are told that these men also brought their girls to Brian's house. But there were three men who weren't going to let Brian go, and so the murder took place. If we examine the derogatory way in which Marty and Joe referred to Brian, invariably as a "rich fag", a "ponce" or a "poof", then we notice that they still subscribe to these opinions today, as if calling Brian by these names somehow vindicates their actions. Neither person in the extracts published in *Blown Away* and *Paint It Black* have expressed any remorse for the part they played in Brian's death, but still hold to the conviction that Brian deserved what he got, and presumably for being a "rich fag".

What we do know is that Brian spent his last night in the company of people with whom he shared nothing in common. He was basically lonely at Cotchford Farm, and in his vulnerable state lacked the authority to prevent the builders staging a party. He was thus a prisoner in his own house. But he was more than that. He was resented, and one might even say despised by the men who had gathered ostensibly to work on his property. It would be a mistake to assume that the way Brian dressed was simply a product of sixties fashion. Even given the androgynous liberality of sixties clothes, Brian took it a stage further and feminized his costumes with scarves and jewellery. He had in the eyes of the public departed even from the permissible wardrobe allowed a pop star. Brian had ceased to make a distinction between his stage and off-stage clothes: and this made him, in every sense of the word, an individual.

Nicholas Fitzgerald implies in his book that the reason Frank Thorogood went indoors to have a cigarette, was that he needed one. He had after all just "done Brian". The builders and their girlfriends had dispersed in a hysterical debacle, possibly giving rise to the screaming which bought Mrs. Hallett out of doors – and there was serious thinking to be done. But that thinking understandably lacked rational premises, and so we are faced with all the glaring inconsistencies in the three statements which Geoffrey Giuliano has so astutely analysed.

Returning once more to Nicholas Fitzgerald's account of his last minutes spent with Brian, before he left the house to go to the station: "I was preparing to leave via the French doors when I saw two men again fiddling with the spotlights at the pool. I pointed them out to Brian and he came up to the window and froze there, glaring at them. 'What the hell are they up to?' he said quietly. 'They should have knocked off work at six. I'm fed up with this. I don't trust them. I'll have another go tomorrow to get the whole mob out of here. I want Spanish Tony instead. I want him here to look out for me.'"

Now Joe in his confession to Giuliano claimed that both he and Frank were given a financial incentive shortly after Brian's death. Joe claims that his payment was intended as an encouragement to keep silent, but he was unclear as to whether Frank's reward was blood money for having killed Brian. If we are to place trust in the latter theory, and that Brian's murder was premeditated, then the spotlights being put up at the pool were probably done so with the intention of better committing the crime. Brian didn't wish to have spotlights over his pool, and we remember that Nicholas was dazzled by the intense light they projected. If Brian hadn't ordered those two spotlights, then someone again was being dishonest with his finances. Major theft was being condoned on Brian's premises.

What seems to have been indubitably established by three fine books on the subject, A.E. Hotchner's *Blown Away By The Sixties*, Terry Rawlings' *Who Killed Christopher Robin?* and Geoffrey Giuliano's *Paint It Black*, is that Brian Jones did not die of natural causes. He was a young man, who even if he had incurred premature liver damage as a consequence of alcohol, would have had every chance of recovering from this condition. Brian's state of health was not terminal. Nor as far as we know did he have any good reason to take his own life. He was, on the contrary, supremely optimistic about his future as a musician, and the band with whom he was working at the time of his death. If events had gone according to plan Brian would have most probably staged a big comeback by December 1969. He would in all likelihood have become a serious chart rival to the Rolling Stones.

Since providing the police with her initial statement, Janet Lawson has remained uncontactable, her whereabouts unknown. She has never been available for comment on what really happened at Cotchford Farm that night, and Anna Wohlin after being sent to stay with Bill Wyman for a week, because he had a Swedish girlfriend, Astrid, was hurried out of the country. Of the three principal witnesses one is dead, one has dematerialised, and one is now writing her account of an apparent murder.

But who were the others gathered at Brian's house that night? Nicholas Fitzgerald observed a man and a woman standing at the far-left of the pool, while three men at the far-right were interfering with the swimmer. Taking into account the man who stepped out of the bushes to warn Nicholas off the property, this makes a count of five men and one woman, independent of whoever else was indoors at the time. This provides us with a total of four men other than Frank Thorogood who were not supposed to have been at Cotchford Farm that night. If we are to believe the official statements, then we are told that apart from Brian Frank Thorogood was the sole male occupant of the house that night. Interviewed by Giuliano, Tom Keylock is adamant that no party took place at Brian's house that night, and that the builders had all gone home by the time Brian drowned. But why on that night in particular should there have been no party at the house, when it was an accepted practice that the builders stayed on and generally abused Brian's hospitality. Why should that night in particular have been different to any other? And because of Brian's manifold social connections, people were in the habit of dropping in unannounced. Drinks and music, the constituents of a sixties party could have been called for at any time. Now if Tom Keylock was not at Cotchford that night, then he must have relied on his friend Frank Thorogood for an account of events. Interviewed by Giuliano in December 1993, Keylock was still insistent on defending his friend Frank Thorogood's honour, despite the fact that Thorogood had confessed to him on 7 November 1993 that it was he who had murdered Brian. Thorogood's confession as it was reported by Keylock to Terry Rawlings, the author of *Who Killed Christopher Robin?*, deletes the statement he provided to the police at the time of Brian's death. It follows that if one of the three key witnesses provided false evidence on the occasion, then the other two witnesses either never saw the murder take place or were complicitous with Frank Thorogood's story.

Events at Cotchford Farm that day, prior to Nicholas Fitzgerald's arrival, had been lively. Suki Potier, Brian's former girlfriend, had arrived to retrieve her remaining possessions, and an argument had broken out between the two about Anna Wohlin's presence in the house. Frank Thorogood had in the meantime gone up to London to pick up wages for himself and his workmen from Fred Trowbridge at his Maddox Street office. It was there that Thorogood heard the news that Brian had requested that all payments to him and his team were to be stopped immediately. If we are to reconstruct possible events, then Thorogood must have returned to Cotchford with a score to settle against Brian.

In the two independent books written specifically about Brian's murder, Terry Rawlings in his *Who Killed Christopher Robin?* adheres to the belief that Tom Keylock was not at Cotchford that night, and that Brian was murdered single-handed by Frank Thorogood as an act of revenge for money owed. The police were to hold Thorogood all night and were initially convinced that he was the man responsible for Brian's death. This view, with the addition of Tom Keylock's added information that Frank Thorogood had confessed to murdering Brian – and do we take this for a truth? – was very much the official view accepted at the time of Brian's death. As neither Janet nor Anna witnessed the murder, according to their accounts, so Frank Thorogood could never be convicted. There is no taped evidence of Thorogood's having confessed to the act, and so we can only rely on Mr. Keylock's reportage.

Geoffrey Giuliano's book *Paint It Black*, like that of A.E. Hotchner's before him, asks questions that are usually better not raised. Giuliano's credibility as an investigative journalist has never been better displayed than in his research for *Paint It Black*. Giuliano even managed involuntarily to have Tom Keylock in a lapse of memory admit to having been at Cotchford that night. "Well I was out there by the pool with him," Keylock confessed, "and went inside for a cigarette. When I came back three minutes later he had drowned." But wasn't this precisely what Frank Thorogood claimed? He too was to admit to having left Brian swimming alone in the pool, and to have gone indoors for a cigarette.

Nicholas Fitzgerald had been forcibly ejected from the farm at 11.15 p.m., having presumably watched Brian in the process of being drowned, and yet the police only received a call from Cotchford at 12.10 a.m. If we are to believe Nicholas's accuracy in time keeping, then there is a period of almost fifty minutes for which to account. What happened in this approximate time? Mrs. Hallett claims to have heard an exodus of cars soon after she was alerted to a voice or voices screaming from the vicinity of Brian's pool. In the unaccounted for fifty minutes prior to the police being contacted in East Grinstead, alibis if such were the case could have been hurriedly constructed, and Brian robbed of the considerable amount of cash that he had informed Nicholas he kept concealed in the house.

The whole conundrum of Brian Jones's death remains an enduring mystery. According to Brian's gardener, Michael Martin, "some evil men got hold of him and they just wouldn't let go." Brian was to die in the same month as the Rolling Stones filed a 29 million dollar lawsuit against their manager Alan Klein, a case which was to be settled out of court in favour of the Stones. Brian's promised pay-off settlement of £100,000 had failed to be honoured.

Keith Richards in speaking much later of his personal enquiries into what happened that night observed: "I got straight into it and wanted to know who was there and couldn't find out. The only cat I could ask was the one I think got rid of everybody and did the whole disappearing trick so that when the cops arrived, it looked like it was just an accident." In a purely social context Brian's death, like those of other sixties rock icons, Janis Joplin, Jim Morrison and Jimi Hendrix, appeared to morally address the issue of a generation which had exceeded its limits. To a disapproving establishment Brian's death seemed to be the logical outcome of an aberrant lifestyle: there was a consensus of feeling that Brian deserved what he had got.

Brian was to many of those who loved him the most gentle and sensitive of beings. That he was unreliable and emotionally traumatised by an unsympathetic upbringing were also conditions of his character. He was above all too young to have done the serious inner work on himself which comes as the psychological reward of maturity. Brian is too often judged as if his life was rounded and complete, rather than angular and half-formed. And yet in those intensely lived twenty-six years, Brian had set in motion a fast-forwarded process of individuation. From an unexceptional Cheltenham background and without parental or educational encouragement he had evolved as one of the most talented musicians of his generation with a dress sense that placed him as the leader of androgynous fashion. Far more than Mick Jagger, it was Brian Jones who became the symbol for the great psychosexual changes characterised by the 1960s. Pat Andrews has reminded me of how Brian chose to plant shocking-pink azaleas and rhododendrons at Cotchford, and of his concern as an early environmentalist to raise trees on his property. Brian's love of pink azaleas separated him in sensibility from the coarse workmen at Cotchford intent on exploiting his vulnerability. Brian should never have been subjected to the situation in which he found himself. He was surrounded by the type of men who by way of reprisals for being found out in criminal acts threatened to "rearrange faces". The whole conspiracy was still another instance of a feminine man being ruthlessly persecuted by an instinctually aggressive machismo. Everything about Brian's nature disliked confrontation. It had been the root problem in his fearing to submit his songs to the other Rolling Stones, and at Cotchford he felt unable to confront the brute force of men who were potentially physically dangerous. The financial drain made on him by Frank Thorogood's extortionate demands for work done badly or not done at all should surely have been stopped at source: the Rolling Stones organisation. Meanwhile, Thorogood's unreal estimates were being approved by his friend Tom Keylock. After Brian's death the merciless theft continued. Not only were his priceless clothes made into an unauthorised pyre, but his house was looted of valuable antiques and his personal effects spirited away. Brian's father denies giving the authorisation to have his son's clothes burnt, and there is something deeply incriminating implied by this act. It is said that after Brian's death, and before the police had arrived at the farm, his master bedroom was stripped of its sheets and bedding. The ritual burning of Brian's clothes, an extraordinary act of violation in itself given their value to posterity, may simply have been a cover for the more important incineration of sheets.

Whatever happened at Cotchford Farm on the night of 2 July 1969 was a violent offence against spirit. Brian, like most anxiety temperaments, feared death in the way that youth does, for his individual destiny was incomplete. Brian undoubtedly died in a state of terrible panic. The violation to his luminous karma and exquisitely attuned sensitivity was like smashing a flower with a hammer. He was furthermore killed on his own property where he, more than anybody, had the right to act and do as he wished. The recriminations brought against him by the likes of Joe and Marty that Brian treated them with arrogance does nothing to take into account the fact that Brian was distracted by anxieties, often unwell at the time and preoccupied with affairs of his own. He was murdered for base reasons which carry with them no moral or spiritual redemption. Many believe that Brian's spirit lives on as a radiant entity. The seventeenth century poet Henry Vaughan had a vision in which he relates: "I saw Eternity the other night,/Like a great ring of pure and endless light,/All calm, as it was bright." Perhaps this is the inviolable precinct from which Brian now transmits psychic energies. The tragedy of life is that we can never return twice the same. Brian was denied the fulfilment of his incarnation as a gifted musician. After his death the swimming pool at Cotchford Farm should have been filled with roses. As it is, those who were guilty of taking his life continue to carry on with their normal occupations in the belief that they are triumphantly free.

Marc Almond: The Last Star *Jeremy Reed*

The Last Star is the best-selling, in-depth account of career of Marc Almond. Author Jeremy Reed traces the evolution of Almond's music and lyrics from the legendary Soft Cell, through his various solo records and collaborations, to his late emergence as perhaps the greatest male torch singer of his generation.

The result is a sympathetic and vivid portrayal of a controversial, enigmatic modern star living and working at the creative edge of his art.

With 24 pages of photographs

"Shapely, salty and sexy." – Loaded

NEW EXPANDED AND REVISED EDITION

ISBN 1 84068 006 7   £11.95/$17.95

Scott Walker: Another Tear Falls *Jeremy Reed*

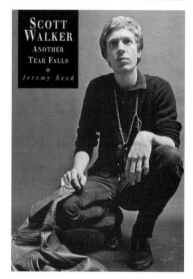

Jeremy Reed's highly original study of Scott Walker finds him engaged in the assessment of a singer who has grown to become a contemporary legend. Walker's inimitable voice first graced the pop charts in 1965, and the short-lived Walker Brothers embraced a popularity comparable to that of the Beatles or Rolling Stones. As a solo artist, Walker quickly achieved international acclaim and recognition with the classic set of albums *Scott 1–4*. But the singer's antipathy to media exposure, and to live performance, gradually led to him becoming a virtual recluse.

In *Another Tear Falls*, Jeremy Reed charts Scott Walker's progress from chart sensation to successful solo singer to the rarely-glimpsed enigma with a sensibility ill-suited to stardom, whose innovative albums *Climate Of Hunter* and *Tilt* were critically acclaimed as recent masterpieces. With a passionate empathy for his subject's life and work, Reed succeeds in bringing a poet's vision to his evocation of one of the most original voices of all time.

With 16 pages of classic photographs

ISBN 1 871592 75 7   £11.95/$17.95

Brian Jones: The Last Decadent *Jeremy Reed*

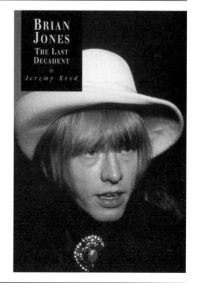

Brian Jones, rock'n'roll godstar, founder member of the Rolling Stones, the murdered androgyne whose fragile psyche was ultimately broken by an industry which, nonetheless, provided him with the means to luxuriate in the bizarre and unorthodox.

Jones's alcohol and drugs excesses, his tormented and often psychotic states, his dandified propensity to cross-dress, his love of literature, privileged background and refined speaking voice all placed him in the decadent tradition, the last of a rarefied aesthete's lineage.

In *The Last Decadent*, Jeremy Reed vividly recolours Brian Jones's brief, but incandescent and extraordinarily subversive life amidst the pop and fashion whirlwind of the Sixties, and in doing so presents perhaps the most illuminating and evocative portrait yet written of a fallen rock'n'roll angel.

Includes 16 pages of classic photographs

ISBN 1 871592 71 2   £11.95/$17.95

Ordering details: www.creationbooks.com

Creation Books International
http://www.creationbooks.com
UK office/mail order sales:
83, Clerkenwell Road, London EC1R 5AR
Tel: 0171-430-9878 Fax: 0171-242-5527
E-mail: info@creationbooks.com
US office/mail order sales:
PO Box 11663, Berkeley, CA 94712
Tel: 510-540-7937
*Creation products should be available in all proper bookstores; please
ask your local retailer to order from:*
UK & Europe: Turnaround Distribution, Unit 3 Olympia Trading
Estate, Coburg Road, Wood Green, London N22 6TZ
Tel: 0181-829-3000 Fax: 0181-881-5088
Benelux: Fringecore, Meibloemstraat 30, 2600 Berchem, Belgium
Tel: 03-239-6770 Fax: 03-281-3389
E-mail: dee@fringecore.com
Italy: Tarab Edizioni, via San Zanobe 37, 50129 Firenze
Tel/Fax: 055-473515
USA: Subterranean Company, Box 160, 265 South 5th Street, Monroe,
OR 97456
Tel: 541-847-5274 Fax: 541-847-6018
US Non-Book Trade: Last Gasp, 777 Florida Street, San Francisco, CA
94110-0682
Tel: 415-824-6636 Fax: 415-824-1836
Canada: Marginal, Unit 102, 277 George Street, N. Peterborough,
Ontario K9J 3G9
Tel/Fax: 705-745-2326
Australia & NZ: Peribo Pty Ltd, 58 Beaumont Road, Mount Kuring-gai,
NSW 2080
Tel: 02-457-0011 Fax: 02-457-0022
Japan: Tuttle-Shokai, 21-13 Seki 1-Chome, Tama-ku, Kawasaki,
Kanagawa 214
Tel: 44-833-1924 Fax: 44-833-7559